To JAN & JERRY
my new friends

J Caprim

with best wishes

Voice from the Mountains

Prelare m. 920 col Monte Vettore m. 2478

Voice from the Mountains

Anthony Caponi

NODIN PRESS

ISBN: 978-1-935666-01-1
Design: John Toren

Library of Congress Control Number: 2010924712

Nodin Press, LLC
530 North 3rd Street
Suite 120
Minneapolis, MN
55401

To my children I dedicate a true story
In the hope of touching the common ground
Where humanity is rooted and from which
Creative energy branches out
Always reaching toward the light
Always anchored to the ground.

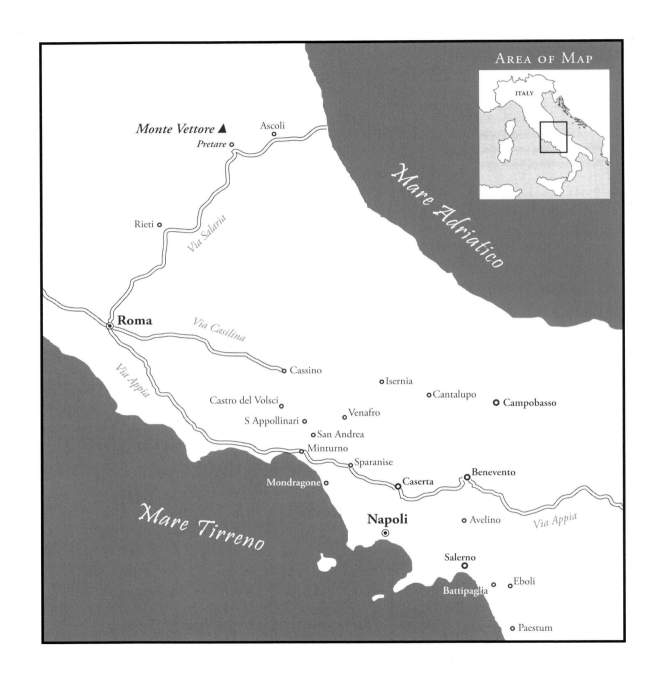

AREA OF MAP

ITALY

Monte Vettore ▲   Ascoli

Pretare

Rieti

Via Salaria

Mare Adriatico

Roma

Via Casilina

Via Appia

Cassino

Isernia   Cantalupo   ● **Campobasso**

Castro del Volsci

Venafro

S Appollinari

San Andrea

Minturno

Sparanise

Benevento

Mondragone

Caserta

Mare Tirreno

Napoli
◉

Avelino   *Via Appia*

Salerno

Eboli

Battipaglia

Paestum

From a distance of a lifetime and many choices
I circle and return to what I was born
where children dug clay from torrent banks to play at making things
without reference to art or talent.
I return to the place of pleasure where labor blended with songs,
where every soul was audience and performer.
There, amid the rocks of time, the church, the school and home
combined to shape my self-shaping thoughts while, unsuspectingly,
a mountain imprinted its stone in my aesthetic innocence.

No road led out of town.
No cause brought in strangers
In the middle of winter.
All around—mountains.
Within their folds—the village,
Covered with snow and innocence.

I

A Voice from the Mountains

I owe less to words than to the flavor of their voice.
I owe to the songs I heard from the cradle.
I owe to the mountains that enclosed the narrow valley
where peasants worked the fields and sheep kept the lawns,
where children played and picked mushrooms.
I owe to the unspoken philosophy that connects mind to the working hands
and regards the sweat of labor as the seasoning of the soul.
"The steeper the slope the less I need to stoop,"
said grandfather, as he planted potatoes one at a time
on the lower slopes of a mountain.
Pride and self-respect showed in the manner he flung his sweat
from his brow to the ground with a sideswiping of his hand.

Though I count my years from 1921,
I was born in the Middle Ages, in a village lost in time
and nearly forgotten in a narrow pass of the Apennines.
There, life was simple and sure.
The future was eternity.
The past was inscribed on tombstones.

≈

A cluster of houses abutting each other, cemented to the slopes of
Monte Vettore, was Pretare—the place of rocks, my native town.
From this vantage point the world looked right,
and what the people saw was not open to doubt.
The sun rose on the morning side
and settled reliably on the western heights,
as each day re-enacted the spectacle of creation.
Faith was the sure expectation that winter and spring would arrive in proper sequence
to allow the seeding of crops, a time to work and harvest, a time to play and rest.

Tilting toward the sun on a lower slope of the mountain,
the village lit up in the morning, one roof at a time,
emerging from the night as an extension of my dreams.
The amber of baked clay reflected in my room the glow of a new day.
A mountain took shape at each awakening,
filling my view with a weather-shaped monument.
A donkey brayed and the town began to stir.
The cattle left their stalls and headed for the pasture.
The tillers walked alone on different paths, carrying their *bident*
on one shoulder, the way a hunter carries his gun.
A shepherd whistled his two-fingered commands to the barking dogs.
The sheep bleated their confusion in a variety of voices,
mounting in a crescendo as they passed the house.
They crossed the water ditch and soon the town grew quiet.

Monte Vettore bore the village on its lap
Much like a mother sitting with parted legs
Holds her baby in the hollow of her skirt.
Hills leaning on hills extended from the mountain's sides,
Curving around the town as robed arms,
Dipping their massive folds toward the valley.
A clear-water stream marked the town's limits on one side.
A torrent drained the mountain on the other.
Each sculpting a trench in virgin stone,
They followed the contours of the valley
And merged in one stream
Where the mountain completed its cradle,
Where the village began its climb
In an uphill world that ended in the sky.

Few of the townsfolk spoke Italian understandably or willingly.
Italian was the language of respect used with strangers and teachers.
The things that were fun to say—the long tales before a fireplace, superstitions,
folk wisdom and humor—could only be conveyed in local *Pretarese.*
Some beautiful expressions were not translatable into another language, because the
meaning did not belong to the words, but to the thinking of the people using the language.
Even God had his own language.
In church and at home prayers were recited in Latin.
No child, no adult, besides the priest, understood the words
but everyone was sure that God did.

≈

The bell tower was the tallest thing in town.
Just the cross above could reach Heaven!
The slender structure
Enclosed nothing but stairs,
Unless it was the heart of the village.
All that mattered was its reach toward the sky.
If it had a door it didn't open on the street.
No window looked in or looked out,
Except near the top where two bells hung
From the raised brow of twin arches.
The only other thing the tower held high
Was the stare of its marble-faced clock
That kept time in Roman numerals
And gave it out in heartbeats.
A large bell rang out the hours.
A smaller voice echoed the quarters
Between the hills of the narrow valley,
To tell each soul when to eat and when to work,
To remind the fearful that night was coming.
Over their cradle and over their casket,
The countdown continued:
One at a time, two hinged hammers
Pounded the solemn bronzes,
Each time recounting the previous total and adding
One.
A man in the fields folded his hands
On an upright hoe, and there he put his chin.
Nodding his head he finished the count, then
Spit in the hollow of his grip
And leaned forward,
Satisfied that eternity was accounted for.

≈

Built of the same rock it stood on, Pretare blended with the mountain
and together they aged with the world.
Few homes showed the white of new mortar.
The villagers found dignity and comfort in old age.
They valued structures and people that signified endurance.
On this rocky site, a home was not sold or bought.
It belonged to the family and the ghosts of relatives.
Homes were known by family names and families were known by where they lived.
The priest, once a year, entered each abode to sprinkle holy water
on walls and people; to bless food and furniture, stalls and animals.
The whole town was one blessed household, where everything stayed in its proper
place and everyone knew where everything was.
In this stronghold, people were bound as loyal *paesani*.
They walked the streets as family members and assumed that any adult
was to any child protector and parent.

"Pretare is much older, much much older than any other village in this part
of the world," said my mother, as one uttering the highest criterion of respect.
"Our modest town was once a great city, known as *Belfiore*,
before the rock slide buried it under."
There was no record of such a city and she offered no evidence.
Pronouncements by the elders required no proof other than constant repetition.
Legends were as valid as history, as real as the she-wolf that nursed Remus and Romulus,
as true as Rome itself. Besides, the sloping valley abounded with signs of an ancient catastrophe.
Boulders bigger than buildings were still poised in their rolling stance, and where the last rock stood,
another town began, appropriately called Piedilama—end of the rock slide.

No peasant's status was ever so humble that he couldn't look down at someone less
endowed than himself.

Out of sight and out of grace, though only one kilometer downhill from Pretare,
the people of Piedilama were the butt of our jokes.
Pinched between the hills that enclosed the valley,
Piedilama seemed to serve no greater purpose than to validate our better fortune.
Malice or compassion had nothing to do with our patronizing view of the Piedilamesi.
Malice is the expression of a resentful loser.
Compassion is the self-identification with the plight of a fellow human.
Neither emotion applied to the scorn evoked by our remote neighbor.
A good mule, a good dog, was easy to respect, but a *cafone* was not just an ignorant,
poor peasant; he was a dim-witted, two-legged animal who had lost all concerns for
how others viewed him.
He couldn't be hurt. He couldn't be pleased. He had no pride.

Like people who had known better days, the *Pretaresi* were proud beyond their means.
They ate polenta and corn bread in the privacy of family. They saved white bread for guests.
The whiteness of the bread was the measure of affluence and status.
It was important for one's self-esteem to feel rich in the presence of strangers.
We were all poor, but nobody told us to feel poor.
We didn't know there was a lack of anything essential to happiness.
Nobody was ever so hungry as not to appreciate his appetite.
It was no one's fault that the land was mostly gravel,
with not enough trees to provide firewood to heat our homes.
There was plenty of water at the public fountain and when, in winter, it froze
in its containers, one could hardly blame nature for behaving naturally.
Living, for the peasants, was not different from playing *Scopa*.
One played the cards he was dealt the best way he could.
When water became ice, it was immensely more important to keep warm than wash.
Besides, "Only dirty people wash every morning."

Stale bread, soaked in water, revived with salt and olive oil, was a modest meal for a growing boy. Even so, if asked, I was to say, "I ate meat and spaghetti."

The family had to save face.

No self-respecting person would suggest that his share of life was less than enough.

HUMILITY and PRIDE were not contradictory terms.

Humility was a private concern. Pride was a necessary, public image.

True, some people had more than others, but enough was enough.

Pride was the social equalizer. It gave scope and purpose to life.

It prodded the mind to be resourceful. It gave the spirit endurance.

We, the peasants, used none of these words but, all of it, we understood.

The only copy in town of the national newspaper was mailed to the priest. He would, at times, share its contents with a small group of men with whom he also shared his wine.

He read the printed words, then reread between the lines, with the ease of a practiced translator.

Everyone in town knew there was a great difference between the WORD and meaning!

It was common practice to say *"Favorisca"* to any stranger who happened to enter a home at dinner time, even if there was no food to be shared.

It was mandatory to answer *"No, grazie,"* even if the speaker was hungry.

Everything said had a function, but one didn't listen to the words to determine what was meant.

We knew that the mouth accommodates hypocrisy with words and smiles.

It is the rest of the body that speaks honestly. The voice, the hands, the eyes—all together rarely synchronize with a lie.

∿

A cluster of homes clung to each other, like the swallows' nests cemented on their
walls, following every slant and ledge of the uphill site.
In such a setting I recall my home—a two-room castle, entered by way of a concrete
ramp that, like a drawbridge, spanned a sunken road where sheep passed to enter their
stalls under our living space.
The door to our house was seldom closed.
It was the main source of light for the kitchen.
The kitchen served as hallway to the bedroom where a window let in daylight and
emitted from the room the refuse of the night.
Between the two rooms, a bare electric bulb hung by an extra length of wire.
At suppertime it was rehung over a small table where, at eye level, I looked with wonder
at the dim filaments of a three-candle bulb, not knowing then how deeply they would burn
into the emulsion of my memory.

Having promised fidelity "for richer or poorer," my father brought his bride to the
two-room house.
Their nuptial bed was a heap of cornhusks contained in a bulky sack called *pagliaccio*—
what in former days was filled with straw.
Set on wooden benches high above the floor, the big sack had two slits on each side
through which, every morning, Mamma reached in the full length of her arms to ruffle
the matted leaves into a buoyant nest.
On this pile of leaves I was conceived. And before Mamma's belly showed,
Father left for America.
I was nearly four when he first returned and, before I got to know him, he left again.
I saw no connection between his coming home and my brother being born.
I remember Mamma sitting with parted legs before the fireplace and a kitchen full of women
making noises and taking turns putting me back to bed every time they caught me snooping.
When I awoke in the morning there was Mamma, me and baby brother.

Resentful that Mamma was staying in bed with a stranger, I stood on the cedar chest to
watch the snow fall while banging my nose on the windowpane.
An impulse unlatched the two louvers and let the wind blow them open
and let the winter in the room.
Satisfied by Mamma's outcry, I left in search of Grandmother.
She was in a nearby home, knitting and talking with other women,
in their usual way of passing a cold day.
In winter the men gathered in taverns. The women got together with neighbors,
taking turns at sharing home and fireplace to save firewood and make of chores a
shared pleasure.
"Nonna, you better come home!" I said with a concerned voice, but not yet ready
to tell her why or admit I cared.
I nagged and pulled at her skirt until she decided on her own,
"It's time I check on my daughter and baby."
From a distance Nonna saw the open door. Directly in line was the open window
and part of the bed covered with snow.
When I saw Nonna run I was relieved.

What I didn't know of my own infancy I learned by watching Mamma care for baby brother.
The swaddling of the baby into a stiff, elongated package was to give him "a straight body."
The urine soaking through the bundle was no reason for undoing it.
The wetting was nature's way of disinfecting its creature.
Before the warm light of burning logs, Mamma and I sat in the evening for the ritual
unwrapping and merrymaking.
Going around and around the small body, Mamma undid the swaddling by rerolling
the long strip of cloth until she had freed the kicking legs.
Tipping her lap and baby forward, she washed my brother with warm wine.
She scooped her hand in a wide pan and let the wine dribble off the naked baby.
What spilled on hot ashes boiled up as sweet-smelling vapors, wrapping the small family
in a magic mist of pleasure.

Slowly and softly, Mamma sang her songs with the rocking of the cradle, as I repeated her words and motions to get the feel of love's sharing.

What Mamma demonstrated she also said:

"These are the songs I sang for you, my first-born.

Your brother is of your flesh and you are both of my body."

Thus a child learned to see himself in another person as he rocked the cradle and sang the words, "your happiness is my happiness."

Mamma never explained people's mutual needs—the pleasure of giving and receiving.

She expressed a basic truth from the depth of her love and direct experience:

"When my breasts ached I knew you were crying, and I would come home from the fields to make us both feel better."

"I nursed
You for sixteen months, and when I tried to wean
You, you tore my blouse.
You refused egg yolk and anything I chewed.
You were stubborn from the beginning!
You were my first born and I couldn't refuse
You. Nonna Susina took you to her house but without
You knowing, I came at night to hear
You cry from under the window, outside.
I suffered double pains.
Your want oozed from my body. I pulled at
My aching breasts and cried at
Your crying.
Your brother is a second born.
I'll nurse him only fifteen months."

Nonna Marianna was the widowed grandmother on Father's side.
She had her own room in her own house but took her meals at our home.
She had three married sons who took turns, one month at a time, to provide for her basic needs.
She was the matriarch and final judge on the performance of her three daughters-in-law.
From her, I learned how to eat politely by taking a little bite of cheese and a big bite off the bread.
The small portion of cheese was to last me until I had filled my belly with the more plentiful food.
She showed me how to drink water by dipping a ladle in the *conca* and not throwing the leftover back
in the container.
But I taught myself how to drink left-handed so not to put my lips where she had.

Nonna Susina, on Mamma's side, was mother to eleven and Grandmother to all.
"He is twice my son!" she reminded Mamma when forbidding her to scold me in her presence.
Playing in puddles and going home with wet feet was enough reason for a spanking.
It was a good reason to stop first at Nonna's house where she showed me how to dry my shoes
by putting hot ashes in and out of them until the ashes no longer stuck to the leather.
Other than that, Nonna showed me how to love.
More than words, I remember her reassuring voice as she took me into her arms
and pressed in me the touch of security.

Anthony Caponi 30 July 1944
ITALY

Nonna Marianna

I dried my feet in warm ashes
While Nonna
Roasted chestnuts and
Told me I was born
Before "this fireplace."
(She knew! Because Nonna
Was twice my mother,
And her face was honest
As a driftwood shape.)
Letting her voice soften
The screams of that night
When my brother was born,
I watched
The color of burned blood
Darken the shells of chestnuts
Crowded in a punctured iron pan
That Nonna held over the flames
Like a warped crown of thorns.
Moaning, tiny voices leaked
From the swelling seeds.
The pent-up urge to bloom green
Exploded violent blanks,
Ejecting hot pain with the flames,
Retaining the sweet, calmed flesh.

In the stillness of cooling ashes
I watched Nonna
Crumble the burned crust
Between the mill of her hands,
Moving like the great granite wheels
That ground the grain of "daily bread"
To fill burlap sacks with "God's body,"
Warm and moist with revived sweat.
Having shed its purgatory vestment,
I saw the golden heart
Held in her fingers like
A consecrated wafer nearing my lips.
I knew then, as a child knows,
That God's love had the wrinkles
Of Nonna's face and His body the lines
Of newborn babies,
Driftwood, mountains, and seeds.

∼

With unencumbered innocence we, the children of the mountains, understood without reference to reason or words.

No one tried to explain the imposing reality of Monte Vettore.

No one offered to take apart knowledge and make of a mountain a gravel pit of words.

We were born to meaning.

We were born of the world to grateful parents who embraced a child as the embodiment of love and God's gift of life.

We were substance and spirit, creatures and creators.

We touched earth with our barefooted senses and felt as one with the world.

No one taught the peasant child how to think for himself.

He had no choice but to be resourceful.

Lazy questions were not encouraged.

The obvious, was not explained.

The most basic ingredient of my upbringing was a benign neglect.

"A good child does not ask questions!"

Without questions, there was no complicated answer to raise more questions and perpetuate doubt.

Love and security were inherent qualities of family experience. Life's important requirements were not talked about, and one of these requirement was obedience.

The "right" and "wrong" were well within the four commandments relating to God and parents.

The few rules served as boundaries within which we knew freedom.

Life's limitations and God's laws were no more limiting than the surrounding mountains that made of our town a secure nest, from which our spirit took flight.

Climbing hills and picking flowers was a self-sufficient joy.

Only suffering was an incomplete experience requiring a connection to some higher purpose.

The villagers were conditioned to view pain or sorrow as a passing discomfort.

Purgatory, after all, was the way to Paradise.

The pain of childbirth was "God's way" of tenderizing a mother's soul for the greater
love that followed. The labor of coaxing gravel to grow potatoes was inseparable from the
pleasure of feeding a family. I remember hunger as the "good appetite" that predisposed my
appreciation for the plainest of "our daily bread."

The wailing of a mother over her dead child, the clutching and pulling of her breasts, as if
to milk her last drop of sorrow into a wooden casket, was the climaxing of love and life itself.

Under a private sky, overflown by eagles and angels, Pretare reared its young with the touch of
feathers and talons, to tease life with the reality of death and make of living a precious happening.

Like the swift and the fox, the ant and the toad,

every child in town learned to hunt.

I hunted hazelnuts and wild flowers.

Berries and sweet roots I ate on the spot.

Mostly I hunted for a high ledge or a tall boulder

from which to look down and stake my claim.

From an eagle's perch, my hunting territory expanded.

Hills and knolls swelled the landscape with mushroom shapes pushing

their heads upwards through the ground and through each other.

Following the pattern of mushroom hunting,

my eyes leaped from mound to mound,

plucking earth's fruits on the run,

collecting everything through the funnel of my vision.

Mamma taught me some practical do's and don'ts,
but the most fun-things to do, I discovered myself.
At five years of age I visited the tinsmith's dump and brought scraps to the concrete slab
of the old house and with a hammer banged away most of the day.
All that was twisted I made flat. All that was flat I gave a new twist.
I banged on concrete and on the wrought-iron fence that kept me from falling into
a deep underpass.
With a hammer or a stone I shaped things and sounds.
No one asked me what I was doing, and nobody worried.
After all, God himself provided a babysitter.
Every day that a child survived was proof that an invisible guardian angel hovered over him.
What could anyone say to a child who, for hours, kept his head between metal bars to make
music? I had heard better music when the band came to town for the feast of San Rocco but,
like any other unschooled child, I found something special about a sound of my own making,
and a shape I had shaped.

Had I been asked what I wanted to become, I might have answered "a musician," but
nobody asked what I wasn't supposed to be thinking.
A boy was born to his father's trade and the ways of his family.
Only girls had a chance to marry into a better family.
It was the general consensus of the villagers that,
"Once you are born, you have arrived.
You are what you are, and you learn to live in this world, as it is."
I wasn't bound to a fatherly influence. I didn't even know what Father did for a living.
Mamma had opted to build a house rather than have us join Father in America.
For years the building site was my playground.
I built my playhouses with the same materials used to build our real home.
I used adult's tools to imitate masons and carpenters.
I shaped chisels and planes at the blacksmith's shop.
My first toy was a xylophone I made with the tools I made.

≈

A major preoccupation of the villagers was the gathering of enough firewood to last
the winter and some.
In families that owned a mule or donkey, it was a man's job to walk the animal up the
long, winding way, over the horizon and then beyond the pasture to the woods.
The women and children without a man or mule in the house took the shortcut straight
up the steep hill of La Tesa—"too hazardous a way for valuable animals."
It was hard work and good sport to find a dead tree before another did and bring home
a load of "legal" firewood in time to go to school. Uniformed foresters would, at times,
parade a handcuffed man through our streets on the way to jail in the municipal town of Arquata.
We looked on with restrained fear and relief because we all cheated and the authorities knew it.
The law was clear about cutting green trees, but there were only so many dead ones to be found.
The arrested man was only guilty of having been caught doing something that even the priest condoned.

Respect for the cold was more pressing than fear of breaking a law that was intended to
inhibit rather than put a stop to a rightful "wrong."
The moral and legal dilemma never crowded the conscience of a people naturally programmed for survival.
We were intimate with the ways of free animals in their struggle to evade the mighty hunter who
killed for food and sport.
We trusted in God's wisdom for His sporting arrangement in endowing humans with a mortal body
and a cunning mind to protect it.
So, in self-defense, we peasants learned to plan ahead by cutting the vital bark around
a tree to make it legal firewood for the next year.

Invisible lines separated our portion of the woods from those reserved for rival towns,
though we Pretaresi redefined our territory according to real needs.
When we trespassed on the Piedilamesi, they were more disposed to retreat than hold their ground,
but the men from Balzo were known to beat our women caught taking wood from their side of the forest.
Like night raiders, we walked in dark hours to arrive at dawn on the opposite side of our hills.
We knew the woods were too far from home when alien bells announced a new day from Balzo,
as if to remind us we were crowding their space.
Walking a thin line between the law and survival, we carried our burden uphill and did not rest until we gained sight of Pretare.
On our side of the mountains, all paths led home.

Clasping my load with an upward embrace
I pressed a small tree on tender shoulders and
Dragged its length on the downward slopes,
While its top branches swept the trail behind
And nudged me gently forward.
Unlike a donkey carrying the dead weight of
Short logs,
I carried an extra length of springy branches
To span weight and bounce from my shoulders to
The ground
So not to make of a branch a beam
And of my load a painful cross.

∽

Father sent money from America at a favorable exchange.

Mamma bought land to build a new home worthy of an Americani family.

The contractor and masons were from out of town.

The laborers were local.

The men at the rock pit used black powder to blow up boulders into manageable pieces.

The women used their heads to carry the pieces to the building site.

"*Calce!*" "*Pietra!*" the masons shouted.

The women responded by carrying mortar and stones up a wooden ladder, high enough for the masons to take the load off their heads and place it directly on the wall.

Stone by stone I saw the building rise and, under each stone, I still see Mamma's face flushed with pride and hard work, her lips stretched between a happy smile and physical strain, her white teeth locked in determination.

In the hills and rocky places, no wheel or sled relieved the burden of animals and people.

Donkeys carried hay and firewood on both sides of their working saddle.

Men carried their load on one shoulder and shifted the weight from side to side to relieve soreness, one shoulder at a time.

Women carried everything but their baby on their head.

The mode of carrying things was fixed according to gender, animal and rank, according to "God's will," as expressed in the common language. The *conca* was the feminine name for a wide-mouthed water vessel that was to be carried only by women.

It did not balance on a man's shoulder. It spilled water in any manner one carried it, except on the head.

I watched women at the public fountain shape a towel into a twisted doughnut, then place it on the crown of their head and press it down with the large copper vessel full of water.

I saw them walk on uneven cobblestones, steadying their load on a motionless head, while shoulders and hips shifted and weaved with the shock-absorbing rhythm of a responding body.

Upon a landscape of homes and hills that had weathered undisturbed for generations,
a few buildings of freshly quarried limestone stood out, like white daisies sprouting out of season.
Sharing a humble birth and a cultivated pride, the Americani competed with each other to build
the "best" palace for their families.

They misrepresented their own hardships and sacrifices.

They exaggerated their good fortune in "the land of plenty."

The personal monuments they built in the fresh air of their mountain homes did nothing to clear
their black lungs.

They worked in the thick air of rubber factories and in the sunken darkness of coal mines to
build "castles" in thin-air places.

The Americani lived to work. Their families kept on being peasants.

Work and frugal living was a conditioned value.

I, and later my brother, kept on gathering firewood while Mamma prepared the same meals, in
the same kettle, over a new fireplace.

Our new home was a three-story house with seven bedrooms, two kitchens, and a dining
room on each floor.

The wrought-iron balcony, the walnut carved doors, the brass knockers, were a necessary
extravagance to appropriately honor the man who, in providing for them, had spent most of his
life away from home.

Of our new possessions, nothing was a greater source of pride than the large terra-cotta pipe
rising from the ground to the third floor.

We had a toilet for all to see!

But to operate the modern convenience was anything but convenient.

We had to carry water, one *conca* at a time, from the fountain to the house, then up six flights of
stairs to the attic where a galvanized container stood, usually empty.

Out of need and social habit the boys met in groups in the privacy of the deep-rutted torrent.
There we chose a place around a water puddle, undid our pants and squatted.
Thus facing each other, we relieved body and spirit by indulging in mutual confessions of
what we thought, more than what we did.
To emphasize a point or to break a momentary silence, we threw pebbles in the water and
watched the tadpoles scatter.
Higher on the torrent bank, a partially unburied pipe hinted at its function. It aimed in the
direction of the teacher's house and matched the pipe on its wall. We agreed that a teacher should
have a toilet, though we saw no evidence of its use at our end of the line.
We gave up on figuring out how the priest resolved his earthly problem.
We mostly wondered if the girls gathered as we did or if each had her own hiding place.

I was shown how things were grown on trees and vines,
how to prepare the soil for plants and seeds,
but nobody told me how babies were born.
I knew there was something that adults did.
I heard it was bad because it was good.
The priest asked at confession if I had done "dirty" things.
I blushed for what I knew as shame but, mostly, I repented
for what I didn't know the priest meant.
There was no way of knowing!
Those who talked had never done it.
Those who knew didn't talk about it.
When people turned their heads aside, pretending not to see,
I saw dogs with dogs and ewes with rams, showing no shame
in showing how they made pups and lambs.
"Animals are animals!" I was reminded.
"Only people weed the land and cultivate their souls with higher feelings."

≈

Some say,
"The sun rises in the morning."
Others explain,
"It doesn't move at all!"
I have no quarrel with those who "know"
Or with those who believe it's so.
From my valley
I saw the sun pour its gold
On the highest peak across the sky,
And watched it spill, slowly, and evenly,
Toward the valley's west side.
For years I have known the time of morning
By the scars on the mountain's face,
As the light, on good days, came down
And washed it clean.
When a heavy sky sagged to the ground,
The mountain rose through the clouds
And kept its head in brighter light.
I have since outflown its eagles and
Looked down on the other side of rain
To see the sun and other stars
Undiminished above the storm.
Even now, the massive boulder
Grows indifferently flat
Against the glow of sunset
And casts upon the village
The shadow of night.
Yet, I know! From what I have seen:
It isn't the sun that comes and goes;
It is its shadow that fills the valley;
It is the night, receding with the tide,
That uncovers the golden-lit mountain
With each unveiling of day

Bound to the soil, and yet so near the sky, the mountain folks enjoyed close connections between the here-and-now and the afterlife.

A narrow bridge spanned the deep torrent that separated Pretare from the Holy Grounds, where rows of marble slabs overlooked the town as white-mantled sentries between the known world and the beyond.

The cemetery was a practical family album, where children toured graves to read names of family members. To the elders, it was a place of weekly pilgrimage—a spiritual exercise of progressively longer visits, to pray and prepare for the inevitable stay.

Contemplation of death was an integral part of living.

It gave reality full weight and meaning.

The faithful didn't believe in superstition. Ghosts and fear were real.

It was proper to acknowledge the wandering souls that crossed the bridge at night to repay family visits in the guise of moths circling light bulbs or as invisible relatives opening creaking doors.

The supernatural was beyond the words of reason.

To believe was a higher virtue than to doubt.

It wasn't words that moved the spirit of peasants.

It was their spirit that moved the words to songs.

It was the music that moved their feet to dance,

re-energized their souls and tired bodies.

"We are the best dancers of the mountain people," said Nonna Marianna.

"We were instructed in the art by the Sibylline fairies who in olden days descended from Monte Vettore to sing and dance on our cobblestones. It is true! Because under their long skirts, instead of sandals, they danced on goat feet. Your uncle had the strength of four men and earned double wages for his labor. He was a sorcerer, they said, and healed people with the touch of his hand."

I believed her then and I believe her still, for

I have looked into the eyes of despair staring back from the debris of a doubting mind.

I have seen the sick gulping drugs and potions while their body yearned

for the healing touch of a sure hand.

The peasants were wise in their simple, practical ways.
They prayed to be spared from the eternal fire,
more than for the promise of heaven.
If given a choice, they would have opted for their present life,
where heaven and hell shared equal time,
giving beauty and truth their full dimensions.
They knew that cold winters contributed to love and human fulfillment
among the people around a fireplace.
They knew how the chill at their shoulders gave greater warmth
and beauty to the flames.
The good and the bad, the verbal separation of understanding,
found unity in the hearts of the mountain people

To see the villagers gathered in one place,
groomed and resplendent in their best clothes,
to compare the best faces in a multitude of choices,
to be seen and acknowledged by others,
one went to church on Sunday.
One learned to give proper reasons for going
but, straight from the heart,
God's love became most tangible in the beauty of his best creatures.
For the elders and the fearful of eternal damnation,
there was an earlier Mass to confess and take communion.
For the others, the priest, in God's name, made allowances.

The church was the pattern and the principle by which the social order was structured.
God—the Father and the Son—sat in judgment on the top circle of the domed heaven.
The Holy Spirit kept in touch with the world through the Pope and his priests, and
through man, whom he had created in his own image and made lord of all living things.
Woman, God cloned from the rib of man, as an afterthought.
The layman ranked only a notch below the priest.
Even in church, a man asserted his dignity by only partially kneeling.
With one knee on the floor, he used the other knee to brace his upright arm that supported the
forehead in the palm of his hand, as if to contain the immensity of his manly concentration.
Worshiping was a female thing to do. Still atoning for the sin of Eve, on the hard floor of the
central nave, a woman knelt piously on both knees. With head hung low in the shadow of her
veil, with chin on chest and nose almost touching her clasped hands, a woman made manifest
before God and man the composure of a true penitent.

Families walked together on their way to church,
and there they parted to take their proper place in God's house.
Women and children filled the bare floor of the large nave.
The only pews, on the side aisles, were private property
to be occupied only by the owners—the town's elite,
who usually arrived late to attract the attention of lesser souls.
Men had their own way of gaining distinction.
Those who chose to be late and wished to be first out,
stood by the baptistery, overlooking the whole scene from behind.
Most of the men entered the church through the sacristy,
where the priest dressed and, like the priest,
entered solemnly, in full view of the congregation.
They circled the apse and chose a place behind and on either side of the main altar.
Thus, eminently positioned on God's stage,
the men appeared to be above worldly sins, as the priest confronted the veiled congregation
and invoked "Our Lord, the Father."

The priest's power extended beyond the church.
His word commuted sentences, prevented incarceration and
kept some men from serving in the army.
Though he kept in sacred confidence what he knew of everyone's sins, it was enough that
everyone knew he knew.
Before the civil authority or in regard to a job application in the city, a man was good if the
priest said he was.
He was bad if the priest said nothing.
Women had nothing to lose but their reputation and,
from what I perceived, that was always in jeopardy.
A statue on a side altar showed the Virgin Mary with her foot on a serpent,
as a reminder for women to resist the Devil's temptation.
No wonder so many women were prone to guilty feelings.
I got some hint of the problem when at night they got together
to knit and chat, while I pretended to sleep.
"The priest wanted to know where I keep my hands in bed," said an older woman
then added with a smirk, "I keep them under the sheets." They all laughed.

The villagers were sure that Mimella had inspired the sermon
when Don Luigi preached on superstition and false healers. But when a child cried
from a belly ache, a mother would have sought the Devil if he were the only recourse.
As it was, Mimella answered a mother's plea faster and more reliably than a prayer.
While Mamma looked on apprehensively, the good witch lady held a fistful of wheat against
my belly, then poured the grain in a glass of water and showed Mamma how some seeds floated
upright—a sure sign of indisposition.
With her open hand Mimella resumed touching my area of pain while moving her lips and
mumbling what might have been words.
I take Mamma's word for my recurring pains.
All I remember is Mimella's hand giving me pleasure, and how willingly I uncovered my belly
when Mamma said I wasn't well.

Only women talked about headaches, and Mamma had more than her share.

For what seemed to be a woman's malady, a man was the healer.

He was tall and reassuring, with an equally reassuring nickname—Il Carabiniere.

He took eggs in payment—one, two, or three, depending on the severity of the affliction.

His method of curing a headache was the same as for the evil eye.

The evil eye was the root of most problems.

Il Carabiniere mumbled his secret words while massaging Mamma's forehead and
temples with both hands.

That the cure was effective was unmistakably clear. Even a child could tell how Mamma's mouth
relaxed into a tight-lipped smile under her closed eyes.

At intervals, the man would dip his finger in a cup of olive oil and let the oil drip
in a dish of water.

If the droplets didn't behave properly, he would repeat the massage until he attained
a pair of clear-eyed droplets, floating in apparent good health.

Eager to begin the day, I climbed westward
To meet the sun on its way down and,
Just before I stepped out of the night,
I turned to face sunrise
On a one-to-one basis.
A sun worshiper and ancient rocks
Glowed in the red of primordial fire
As God, peeking from behind the mountains,
Filtered its intimate colors
and lit the eyes of a primitive boy.
Having beheld a re-enactment of creation
While the priest probably snored,
I said "To hell with hell's fire.
What I've seen is fire from heaven!"

≈

On their way to the fields and back to the watering place, cows and sheep, donkeys
and people, crowded the streets of the village.
Bound to each other and to the land, man and beast obeyed the rules of nature that commit
plants and creatures to take from each other and return to life all that one takes—body, spirit
and nourishment.
Even a poor family had its own pig to serve as pet and provide the next year's meat.
Each family had its plot of land terraced against the slopes, below the green pastures,
where the affluent grazed their cows and sheep.
The wolves and their cubs hid in the bushes, not far from the herd. Dogs with spiked collars
kept guard over the lambs destined to be slaughtered in the spring.
A child shuddered at the sight of blood as he learned to hunt with more pride than pity.

THEN GOD SAID, "LET US MAKE MAN IN OUR IMAGE AND LET HIM HAVE POWER OVER THE FISH OF THE SEA AND OVER THE BIRDS OF THE AIR, AND OVER THE CATTLE, AND OVER ALL THE EARTH AND EVERYTHING THAT CREEPS UPON THE EARTH."

The Bible reader did not raise questions of inequity among God's creatures.

The illiterate peasant had neither the word nor the awareness of prejudice.

Outside of Eden,

it seemed right that animals be animals and people be people.

It made more sense to kick a sheep in the belly

than attribute a soul to animals and think of people as cannibals.

There was no logic to a misplaced bias.

Love and compassion were sentiments reserved for the hunter.

The quarry died with purpose.

All domestic animals earned their own keep by rendering a service or fattening for their ultimate sacrifice.

The dog guarded the herd, the cat caught the mice.

The ox pulled the plow, the donkey carried the crops.

Animals with no skills gave milk or eggs.

We had a few chickens sharing the sty with the pig.

One of my chores was to stick my finger in the rear of each bird to determine which one would lay the next day, and separate the layers from the rest, lest they would wander on someone else's yard and benefit the wrong family.

The rooster stood tall to flap his wings.

"He too earns his living," Mamma said.

Her deliberate omission of an explanation was all the more reason why I scrutinized the bird's strange behavior.

I wondered, "Why does the hen run even before the rooster gives chase; and if the hen doesn't want to be caught, why does she stop and lower her trembling wings before the rooster reaches her?"

Children had no liking for dogs roaming the streets as beggars, obeying no man but one.
Cats were the least trustworthy of all.
One never knew who looked from behind the slits of their eyes.
One could not take chances.
There were too many *streghe* in town who took many forms at night.
They usually changed into cats and liked to suck the blood of sleeping infants.
My cousin Carlino kept on losing weight and was surely dying when his mother discovered
the evildoer. She found the cat in the cradle.
The horseshoe behind the door had not deterred the *streghe.*
The family finally resorted to nailing a forked twig on the front door in the guise of horns.
That made all the difference.
At night, the public laundry-shed became a favored gathering place for witches and spirits.
One could hear them hiss and snarl.
They sounded like cats, but the wise took no chances.

Birds were the only living things we kept as pets,
the only creatures we loved and hunted with equal passion.
They were of the land and of the sky. They provoked that part devil,
part angel quality that made us human.
Even as I fed seeds and polenta to my pets, I kept an armed slingshot in my back pocket,
ready to aim at any flying target.
Mostly I made sport of discovering their hiding places and admiring the structure and
camouflage of their nests.
In time I learned to think like a bird and thought I knew what bird built which nest in which
bush or tree.
When I guessed wrong, I concluded there were some dumb birds.
I knew where the quails nested and where the partridges squatted.
I led hunters from the city to where the game was.
My love of birds combined with my love of hunting, stirring the senses in a mounting
excitement that burst in mid-air with a gun blast and an explosion of feathers.

I listened to the city folks because they talked the language of the educated.

They complained about the scarcity of game.

I thought about their thoughts and decided I would repopulate the hills with chickens.

Lenuccia, our neighbor, had more young chickens than she could account for, so each day

I hid a chick in a wooden box and released it far out in the country.

No one paid attention to my carrying one of my wooden contraptions.

Just the week before, some people shook their heads when I nailed a box to a pair of skis

to slide on a grassy slope.

On the fourth day, the chicken coop had become nervously noisy and Lenuccia caught me

by the hair.

She slapped and kicked me, then told my mother.

Mamma slapped and shook me, then made me kiss her hands.

All that for having teased the chickens.

They had no idea of what I had done. I didn't try to explain

because I knew my thoughts were worth a bigger spanking.

Early in the morning, in mid-winter, the town came alive with the screams of the dying.

Our pig in the sty grunted apprehensively, while I wondered how much he understood.

When his turn came,

I knew he knew the men around him meant harm.

One grabbed him by the ears; each of the others grabbed a leg;

and once they had his struggling body on the low wooden platform, they used their knees

and shoulders to pin him down.

The butcher wrapped a cord around the snarling jaws and stuck a long knife through the pig's

neck deep into its body to cause fast bleeding without hitting a vital organ that might have killed

the animal before its fluids had drained and left the flesh tainted with the taste of blood.

I saw it all gush into a copper pot and, before the day was over, I ate *frittelle,*

made of flour mixed in blood.

Accountable only to heaven,
Smoke rose as morning prayers
From the homes of early risers
Whose turn had come
To stoke the fire and boil water
To make ready for the slaughter.
Black silhouettes on trampled snow,
With arms spread like scarecrows, moved
Toward each other in a shrinking circle,
Crowding within, a lump of flesh
Running on short legs from side to side
Until men and beast collided.
A scream scraped the cold sky
And ice crystals filled the air.
The cry of agony shredded pain
Through the bite of twisted jaws.
Man had cut the pulsing jugular
And let a heart pump itself dry.
The man in apron turned aside
And wiped a knife across his belly.
The others, heaving together,
Dipped the creature in scalding water
And shaved the animal off its body,
Baring the blond, human-soft skin.
A flat-bedded sled, the altar,
Was dragged from house to house
As vapor still clung to the warm planks,
Saturated with spilled life;
As, on the underside, icicles formed
And, on the white snow dripped blood.
Beyond the village, a wolf sprang.
One shake of the head
And the hare was dead.
It was meat,
Unabused,
And promptly eaten.

Carved from solid rock on the walls of deep gorges,
the Via Salaria crossed the Apennines to the Adriatic Sea where the Romans got their salt.
From this ancient road, lesser ones branched and disappeared into the hills.
The gravel lane to Pretare we still called the Roman Road, and its length was duly marked with upright stones giving the distance to Rome. The road markers were the only tangible connection between the mountain people and their country's capital.
Except for the few merchants who brought in goods from the city, most of the villagers did not wander far from home.
For the young and the old, the near and the distant were both within sight, and after sundown, distance acquired a new dimension.
The water ditch became the world's margin.
On one side was our town and the living,
on the other side was the cemetery and the beyond.

My reality of time and distance was not a fixed measurement independent of the mind.
Viewing my native town from where I stand, the place was a secure playpen where children played unattended while adults worked on the sloping fields all around.
As I zoom-in on my past, with that part of the mind that allows passion a full measure of experience, I see a child with his face near the ground, exploring the immensity of his world from the point of view of ants.
I recall distance as measured in steps and the frequency of discoveries along the way.
Climbing a hill brought me before another hill to climb, and occasionally I came upon a village that, by all appearances, didn't want to be discovered.
In a country where history and topography encouraged local independence and deliberate isolation, towns were positioned on hills as potential fortresses.
A stranger entered a town as a foreigner enters a new country where people of different dialect and customs are sensitive and protective of their local sovereignty.
In this setting I covered great distances within walking range.

46

Thirty six kilometers, through twisting gullies that permitted only a short view between the steep hills, was an impressive distance to the city of Ascoli. Few people from Pretare visited the province capital, and that they did on rare occasions.

Mamma walked through the town of unfriendly Piedilama on her way to Borgo, on the Via Salaria, where she caught a bus to Ascoli. In the city, she bought beds, full-mirror dressers and other things to furnish our new home in style.

She was a brave woman for daring to match wits with crafty merchants who had no trouble spotting a peasant by her speech, dress and manner. There was nothing improper or illegal for a storekeeper to ask absurd prices in the expectation of bargaining and bluffing until both buyer and seller felt they had won as much as possible from the other. Most peasants were no match for a city merchant who invariably gave in at the moment he thought the buyer was ready to walk away. Then, the merchant would lift his brows and shrug his shoulders in his practiced expression of a loser, resigned to break even, just to make a sale.

The *Strada Romana*—the Roman Road, connecting Pretare with the Via Salaria—might have been adequate for chariots, but when the Firmani Brothers brought a truck to town, it monopolized the road in both directions. This mechanical device, with solid rubber tires and carbide headlights, was a major happening for the Pretaresi.

The starting of this modern conveyance always attracted an audience. Men took turns cranking its motor, while the driver made adjustments from behind the steering wheel until he had found the ignition setting corresponding with the climatic conditions of the day.

Twice a week the truck left for Ascoli at a prescribed time so that parents could remove their children from the main road.

Once the machine started rolling downhill it wasn't easy to stop. People, surprised on the road, scattered like the chickens in all directions. No one complained about the wheeled menace.

The truck brought back goods for the Firmani store.

It brought back the furniture that Mamma bought in Ascoli.

All that happened in Pretare seemed to fall naturally in place as if in accordance with
a master plan, though the only wisdom involved was in the peasant's way of adjusting to
uncontrollable events.
Our new house was finished.
The American economy had collapsed.
Father was coming home to benefit from it all.
Donning our best clothes, our family went to Ascoli to meet the head of the house on
his return from America.
He had not yet seen my five year old brother, dressed for the occasion in a bright red suit
that Mamma had knit with a matching beret.
Even before Father added his foreign clothes to our group, Mamma responded approvingly
to the deserved stares of the city people.
My brightly clad brother and Mamma's green dress outshined the Italian flag against the
city marble.
Our family together, we commemorated our moment of luxury and self-importance with
a formal photograph.

Lined up as rebels waiting to be shot,
Side by side against a white backdrop
Stood father and mother and two wide-eyed boys,
Preparing to face and out-stare the flash
That would bind them stiffly to each other
And commit to the wall the unalterable image
That each had of himself and of the others,
When time stopped between eye-blinks.
Wedging lungs between the ribs of determination,
The nonchalant, the proud, and the perplexed
Sustained their puffed-out chests with expectation,
While the man behind the trigger, smiling,
Ducked his head under a black shirt
To aim and focus and hide his thoughts.

≈

On the first day of school,
I watched my friends climb the straight stairs and disappear in the stone structure from which
no other door led out to suggest a choice or a way of escape.
As an outdoor creature, circling apprehensively an arbitrary enclosure, my thoughts circled
suspicion until the last of my peers had entered the one-room school.
I followed much later, when pride outweighed my dislike for confinement.
Leaning their elbows on the long writing desks, students filled the room, five to a bench,
arranged as pews with an aisle between,
to separate the girls from boys.
Along one wall, on the girls' side, were the only windows;
the only source of light, the only view that bound learning to life.

A teacher was usually a *Signorina,* aloof and different from the rest of us.
She did not mingle or marry.
She had no choice but to live the life of a dedicated spinster.
A teacher was assigned to serve far from her hometown, to discourage her from using the local
dialect that might lead to undue familiarity with the townsfolk.
Besides, the authorities expected her to help in unifying the country under a common language
and convert individuals to a uniform way of thinking about country and Fascism.
My first grade teacher had strange ideas, and seemed to find a wrong in everything I did.
I spit on the floor and the teacher said, "Wipe it."
I used the bottom of my shoe, back and forth, the way men did in taverns and, again, the
Signorina frowned.
She shamed me to my knees and made me wipe the floor with my own smock.
I might have resented her for life, had she not died of tuberculosis before the year was over.

Tuberculosis, an alien disease in this part of the world,

became a subject of compassion rather than a cause for alarm.

No one expected, even a teacher, to confess a curse that only God can will on individuals.

No one blamed the authorities for assigning the *Signorina* to Pretare in the hope that the mountain air might cure her.

The Piermarini family, with whom she boarded, was proud to have the teacher befriend their own daughter. After the *Signorina* died and the Piermarini girl became ill, no one would have expected a mother to reveal the young woman's secret, even when Uncle Rocco asked for her hand in marriage.

My cousin Mario was born a healthy baby before his mother nursed him her cursed milk.

The mother died early, but not before her son's skeleton became warped and his growth stunted.

Thus I remember my first teacher, who made me wipe a healthy spit to wash away her fear and moral guilt.

My first uniform was a black smock with a red stripe on my left sleeve to identify me

as a first grader. Black was the respectable color of the times, worn by widows and priests, students and fascists.

Every boy in class owned a black shirt, a pair of short pants and a tasseled black fez worn once a month to the Black-Shirt Parade at the communal town of Arquata.

Pinned in front of the black hat was *Il Fascio*—an old Roman symbol, consisting of a golden bundle of upright rods with a battle axe on top to signify strength in unity and willingness to fight for the country.

The girls' attire was less somber, with their short black skirts and white blouse uniforms.

Together we marched singing *Giovinezza* and *Fischia Il Sasso.*

Compelled by the cadenza of the patriotic songs, we attributed the validity of the music to the words we sang.

Thus we screamed in a single voice our willingness to die for *Il Duce;*

and while the music lasted, we believed.

A large map of Europe covered most of the back wall.

Though Russia covered most of the map, the teacher only mentioned the smaller countries
as those who coveted a place on the sunny side of the Alps.

The Austrians, the Germans, the French were all assumed to be our natural enemies for no other
reason than the fact they bordered our enviable country.

Facing class was a map of our noble boot, looming large and in varied colors to identify its
regions and provinces.

Its large scale included even Pretare in the densest of the Apennine Mountains.

All around was "Our Sea." To the north, the "God given boundary" separated Italy from the rest
of the world, described as sunless and cold.

Unaware of all the things we peasants didn't have and all the things we didn't understand,
we sang our pride to Mussolini and country.

Following the simple rules of a phonetic language, within a few weeks we learned to write
anything we could pronounce.

We wrote legible dialect while reading correct Italian.

By the second grade, we were literate enough to concentrate on arithmetic and geography.

The teacher used an orange to demonstrate the world is round.

She navigated her finger about it, and called out names of distant places.

From among the explorers, Marco Polo and Cristofero Colombo popped from her lips as
bubbles of pride, as if to ennoble history with some proper-sounding names.

Synchronizing word and finger, the teacher culminated her lesson by poking *Italia*
on the orange's belly.

Battle by battle, through glorious conquests, the greatness of Rome unfolded in third grade.
Ancient Rome was the focal point of heroism and power on which to pattern modern Italy.
The teacher left no doubt that bravery and discipline characterized a worthy man.
Motherhood and sacrifice described a noble woman.
The more sons she reared the greater the gift to her country.
Mazzini, Garibaldi and other Italian heroes were portrayed on our notebook covers above the words: "For all he has given to his country he has not given enough." This left it for the teacher to explain, "No one has given enough, except those who have died a glorious death."
Mussolini was our modern Caesar and we, the black shirts, sang
"We shall bare our swords at your command and follow you with our banners in the wind."

In class, students were united as uniformed comrades before a teacher's authority.
Away from school, the boys disdained team sports in preference to personal contests that resulted in one winner.
Valor or personal honor was both the cause and the aim of every game or scuffle.
Girls were something else!
Though the teacher did not use a double standard in imparting knowledge, it was understood that a boy did not assess his worth in comparison to a girl. I don't remember a boy ever competing with a girl or resenting her intelligence.
Brains, like beauty, were to be admired in a person who, after all, was destined to join a man in marriage and become with him that inseparable unit in which a soul augments another to fulfill love and life.

Among eagles and mountaineers, the rules of life were simple.

The strong prevailed by natural right.

The young were protected; the misfits, God recalled.

Parents taught their children to read the mood of the mountains,

to foretell good weather or storms, to distinguish dogs from wolves, the poisonous from the harmless snakes.

"If you hurt yourself, pee on the wound," said my mother.

"Your body is fully equipped for self-repairing."

Weakness and handicaps were private curses.

Only a few elders conceded poor eyesight.

Aside from an occasional "evil eye" or bellyache that was easily remedied with a few grains of wheat and words of incantation, everybody in town was healthy and strong.

There was no need for doctors. The sick were dead.

I had been told: "Once every generation, death weeds the weaklings at a tender age."

I thought no more of it until "the plague" struck again and took many of my classmates in the fourth grade.

I remember going to bed one evening and awaking in the morning all skin and skeleton.

With a mouth full of tongue and unable to form a word,

I looked at Mamma's face looking down at mine.

With a superimposed smile over her pained expression, she told me

I had lain as dead for forty days.

First to go was my mind as, slowly, the fever burned my body.

I would have died a painless death had not the communal doctor been replaced by a competent one who diagnosed the recurring epidemic as typhoid.

First in line at the source of streams, our town was known for its clean water, filtered through a mountain of limestone.

No one suspected our spring water had washed the gravel under a stable on its way to the public fountain.

Pain and the smell of disinfectant were the first signs of life
when I awoke from death and found myself in a different body.
The mind was still in possession of its self-image of health and pride when I discerned its
precarious link to a humble bundle of fleshless bones.
Held by my parents on both sides, I let my limp skeleton hang by the armpits, so as not to pinch
the nerves of pain between my bones and the bedpan.
Thus helpless, I was reborn, partially grown and partially wasted, from that limbo where a body
loosens the bonds between matter and mind, where a soul teeters between a new beginning or a
head start in the old body.

The hill was steep and wet when the cow lost its footing and tumbled to the bottom.
"It is God's providence," said Mamma. "Now my son will have enough meat to restore his body."
Each family had its own pork, cured in midwinter, to last the year. Fresh meat was seldom bought
or sold, and nothing larger than a sheep was ever slaughtered on purpose.
From a cautious distance, my brother looked with dubious envy as Mamma sat my bones on a
pillow before a wicker chair that served as table for my exclusive meal of steak and wine.
"He needs the meat for his body and the *Marsala* for his blood," Mamma explained to my
brother apologetically.

From what was left of my purged body, a new person took shape.

The straight, brown hair I had lost in bed grew back in dark curls and, under their roots,

fresh air seemed to flow with my thoughts.

The body was slow in regaining its strength.

The mind compensated with increased appreciation for every response of my conscious body.

I was grateful for the mere feel of my weight on the ground.

Everything I handled touched me first and made me aware of my own hands.

I became aware of the God-like power, in every human, to contain a world of matter and spirit,

of meaning and beauty, within the orbit of the mind.

I returned to school two months later and had no trouble catching up with class.

It was clear from our textbooks that "our valorous troops" had won the Great War,

almost single handed, only to miss out on our proper share of the spoils.

"But," we were told, "Mussolini will restore our Roman pride and empire."

I learned my lines well about Rome and duty.

In my last year of school I was made *Capo Squadra* of the *Balilla,*

the town's young fascists.

Five years of school was all that was available or required for country folk.

To be made squad leader seemed a proper way of culminating an education in which patriotism and religion reinforced each other. Both had their heroes and martyrs, both regarded a soldierly death as the ultimate condition for the glory of God and country.

∽

As each day belongs to yesterday and tomorrow,
I belonged to the people of Monte Vettore who, in turn, belonged to history.
In church I pledged my soul to God.
In school I swore to die for my country.
Both promises were recited as printed.
Between the world of God and that of Mussolini, in equally distant Rome,
the people of Pretare satisfied the ritual requirements of both worlds as necessary
parenthesis to their personal freedom and current realities of living.
Outside the realm of words and distant issues,
the peasants retained their basic frame of reference.
TRUTH was a lump of soil held in the palm of a working hand.
SECURITY was the monumental mass of a durable mountain.

≈

To bring a wider view in focus
I sat on a hill and watched sunrise,
Before the light reached the valley
And undid my reason for climbing.
It wasn't climbing in the dark!
I went up there to sit on a choice
Between school and the best of days.
There I had my own rock to sit on
And two giant boulders to sit under.
The rocks had rolled from higher slopes
And came to rest face to face,
Like the folks in town greeted each other,
Kissing cheeks with arched bodies.
It was more like a chapel than a throne
Where I went to sit, just to be alone;
Or just to look down and think
Of things across the valley and beyond.

≈

1932 and still "no work" in America.

Father extended his stay at home by another year.

He stayed long enough to see Mamma's belly grow with his third child and witness its coming into the world.

Before Father's last return, he had become an American citizen,

a fact I had ignored until it hit me in the face:

my new brother was born an American citizen, a contradiction of the obvious.

He was my brother, son of my own parents, born in the same town where God had willed for us to be born and to belong.

Would all this make me part American?

I resisted confusion by convincing myself that I was a Fascist and a modern Roman.

My baby brother Claudio was named after Mamma's father who had died in America.

My grandfather, my own blood was buried somewhere in Pennsylvania.

"That surely must make me part American!" I claimed just to keep my options open.

Mamma was only eleven when he died and knew him mostly from photographs.

Her only brother, Damiano, also died in the Great War.

My middle brother took his name.

Nonna Susina, with no man to care for her, remarried and had nine more children,

five of which survived childhood to become my uncles and aunts.

Mamma's stepfather was the only man I called "Nonno."

Nonna Marianna, my father's mother, was widowed long before I was born.

She didn't remarry because she had three sons to care for her.

As the first born of her first son, I was named after my grandfather Antonio.

My grandfather made charcoal for a living—the clear burning fuel the rich used for cooking and warming their beds.

He traveled on foot to wherever he could find hardwood trees to cut.

He liked to tell that the Caponi family had come from the region of Tuscany.

Much later in my life I came to know of the historic Capponi family in Florence.

I smiled at the thought of how a black sheep from that noble family might have failed to stress the double "P's" when giving his name on settling in Pretare.

Two years of father's presence was not enough time for me to feel close to him.

I was old enough to be uncomfortable on seeing a man I didn't know behave intimately with Mamma.

It also seemed that Mamma, now, had less time to spare for her grown son.

When I developed an earache, no amount of crying brought either parent to my room.

They slept on a different floor to protect the privacy of their nighttime.

In pain and in the dark I walked across town to Nonna Susina's home.

She put me in her bed and comforted me to sleep.

Days later I realized my left ear could no longer hear a sound.

≈

Father went back to America and I was again the man of the house. I had already proven I could carry a man's load in firewood, work the garden and keep the large house supplied with water.

In summer, Mamma rented the extra rooms to the *Signori* who came from the city to breathe our fresh air and recreate their soul.

At times our guests included boys my own age.

They were better schooled and better dressed than I but when we took to the hills I would come back whole and they a mess.

"Your son is intelligent," said one of the elite guests to Mamma, not realizing that, in his discovery, he had expressed an unflattering expectation of us peasants.

Those who joined me in exploring the country had no trouble deciding who should lead and who should follow.

Relatives of the influential Cardinal Gasparri came to vacation at our home.

From Rome they brought elegance and refined manners.

They also brought along a multi-unit contraption that covered the whole dining table.

It was the first radio I had seen.

Every Italian child knew that Marconi had invented what our books still called the "wireless phone."

But this radio had wires going all over the place.

A wire ran into the ground to reach the water of our cesspool.

Wires across the ceiling led to the roof and up the chimney.

The whole thing was an eerie happening: first the loud static, then the garbled languages of distant countries.

From beyond the mountains, the voice of the world had reached Pretare as a benign invader of our sovereign town.

Finishing school in the prime of my secure boyhood provoked no concern or thought about "the future."

I continued carrying firewood and searching the hills for mushrooms.

I did most things as a pleasurable sport, in competition with my own expectations.

"Whatever you do in work and play is worth doing well," was all that Mamma said on the subject.

I was sure the world made available all I needed in life.

The only person I might have envied was the painter who decorated the ceilings in our new home. My admiration became stranded in a small boat floating on the bright colors of its painted reflection.

I watched the painter mix the colors that magically animated birds and flowers.

I watched his arm rise toward the plaster sky with the sure gesture of a man imitating God with his own creation.

Making clay shapes on pedestal-size boulders by the torrent was a popular pastime.

As a group performance, each boy chose his rock and noisily exclaimed joy in his work and that of others until our play climaxed by returning the clay to the torrent.

We played the material the way we sang a song: once it was over, nothing remained but the pleasure of our performance.

A gentleman from the city who was staying at our home intruded on my innocence by asking to keep my drawings and other things I made.

He had an aunt who painted in oil and copied masterpieces at the local museum.

He convinced Mamma that I should study in Ascoli.

At twelve years of age I found myself alone in a strange city.

Mamma left me with a family who had recently moved to Ascoli from a town that shared a side view of our mountain.

Our houseguest had arranged for me to work in a garage owned by his uncle who was also the local representative of the FIAT Co.

It had been decided I should learn to be a mechanic.

Making pictures was "nice" but learning a trade was what my people understood.

Working on cars that moved by horseless power was no small thing for a boy who had carried heavy loads by no other means than his back.

It made sense that I should train to labor with my hands.

To a peasant, his hands were the antennae of the soul.

They were the touch of life, passed from hand to hand, as imprinted by our Maker when he shaped the virgin clay to make Adam.

Down from the mountains, past the narrow gorge, where the hills spread apart like cypress roots before they sink into the flat land—there Ascoli had stood for centuries, as an oasis at the end of a rocky pass, a fortress impeding Rome's passage to the sea.

Once enclosed by the walled city, I felt more sure of what I left behind than what I came to gain.

The more I walked in the shadows of ancient buildings, the brighter my vision of home.

The more people passed me by, the more my soul retreated toward Pretare, leaving my void body to find its way to my new home.

Overnight I became a displaced part of a life I left behind.

Ascoli Piceno - Piazza del Popolo

Doctors and judges, lawyers and engineers who could afford a car, bought a FIAT from the Ciccarelli Brothers. The dealer, in turn, contracted with the buyers to garage their cars under one roof where his mechanics guaranteed the car's continued performance.

With a steady clientele and prepaid services, the mechanics performed with the diligence of a doctor practicing preventive medicine.

In such a place, I changed tires and patched inner tubes—

duties befitting the lowest ranking assistant.

My pay was the privilege of learning a trade.

"*Si Capo,*" I was coached to reply when the chief mechanic called.

The snappy answer clearly signified "Yes, Master."

He was a tyrant and a geniu—qualities that explain each other and justified the respect he enjoyed from the people around.

The highest honor an assistant could expect was to be asked by the *Capo* to hold the light for him while he worked on a special project—a matter of concentration and no talk.

If the light was aimed wrong or directed to his eyes, one had to be alert to catch his soft grunt.

He never asked for a tool but when he needed one and the assistant didn't have one in hand, he was reproached with lifted brows and the upward look of a lizard.

Without lifting his head, the *Capo* let you know you were not paying attention.

No sooner had I qualified to work on motors than I learned about the nastiness of city people. For laughs and for greed, two fellow assistants conspired to torment me by hiding pieces of the motor I worked on.

Acts of jealousy and spite were as common as rats among the poor people that circumstance had crowded within the city walls, alongside the affluent.

Unlike the peasant who competed for self-respect within his own class, the city urchin learned early in life to resent his rich neighbor while hiding his contempt in the humble behavior of an obedient servant.

There was no way I could convince anyone that two such boys could be guilty of wrongdoing. I thought of revenge, as I paid them off to redeem the missing parts with the chestnuts and cookies Mamma sent me.

After a year of training I earned two liras a week—enough to go to movies.

Cinema and comic books were unknown pleasures to non-city people. Their impact of sudden revelation had, in me, the effect of a tasty appetizer before the main meal.

My expanding world was also an escape from my daily frustrations.

I didn't know that movies were American productions with American actors.

Tarzan was a super-real person who spoke Italian as well as could be expected from a savage.

Tarzan exemplified my fantasy of living an innocent life and performing brave deeds amid wild animals, in a jungle wanting to be explored. It was no wild dream!

Mussolini himself was encouraging young people to join the troops already on their way to enforce our right to a colony in Africa.

Though England, France and most of Europe had done it for centuries all over the world, when Italy invaded Ethiopia the League of Nations imposed sanctions.

That united our people behind Mussolini like nothing in modern history had ever united Italians.

At work everyone was asked to search for nonessential materials to aid our war effort.

What happened all over Italy, I saw in *Piazza Roma:* women waited in line to walk on a platform to give up their gold rings to Black Shirt officials and accept steel bands in return.

No married woman dared appear in public unless her hand exhibited the patriotic color of steel.

It was a time of rejoicing and fellowship.

Soldiers and civilians sang the popular refrain, "Oh little black-faced Abyssinian, we shall bring you to the capital of the free."

"Our soldiers are soldiers and, in war, soldiers kill. Otherwise, we mean no harm to those poor savages who are too uncivilized to appreciate our good intentions."

That was the general view of most Italians.

To me, Ascoli was proof of our superior civilization.

Citizens were forbidden to spit on sidewalks and, since our Leader made peace with the Vatican, no cussing was allowed in public places.

Though in Pretare men still urinated against the masonry wall outside their taverns,

Ascoli provided urinals recessed in the exterior of buildings along the city streets.

With steel flaps, hip high, extending from the wall on both sides, the *Ascolani* relieved themselves, discretely, as people passed by without taking notice of the men facing the wall.

I don't know how women managed. None complained.

In school I was reminded to be proud of the laws that ancient Romans wrote on wax tablets, laws the world copied on sheepskins as a guide.

This I thought when looking at the impressive edifice of the City Tribunal just across the street from my place of work.

During trial recesses lawyers came out on the street to instruct clients and witnesses.

They walked and talked while their arms and hands accompanied the hushed words with the gestures of a conductor.

Gossip about a current case made a point to confirm the fairness of our laws:

a young man accused of rape was cleared of wrongdoing when the defense lawyer had a woman demonstrate how, unless she permitted it, no man could part her legs.

At a sculpture studio just around the corner from where I worked, I passed my lunchtime watching artisans cut uniform slabs from a coarse block of sugar-like marble. I watched them recut the manageable slabs in a variety of sizes and shapes upon which a young apprentice incised letters on the buffed side.

The carver, too much my own age for comfort, demonstrated a skill that would have pleased Moses when he committed his commandments to stone.

In the best light, near the open entrance of the studio, an angel emerged from a white cloud, from the hands of a master carver who chipped away the marble as naturally as he licked his upper lip.

In the evening, when I confronted myself to wash, I wished the smudges on my face had the color of marble dust.

When it was my turn to tend the garage on Sunday, I passed my idle hours drawing on paper and on a large blackboard meant for other uses.

Some of the garage patrons surprised me at the board and inquired about my drawings and my future. They suggested I should be doing more important things than work in a garage.

These well-educated and successful people were telling me I should go to school.

In a class-conscious society, I was conditioned to be satisfied with my lot in life.

Being a *studente* was a privilege beyond my reach or right.

Besides, my parents were already paying for my room and board, and Father had not yet found work in America.

I could not be so ungrateful and insensitive as to capriciously change my mind in mid-course for a more costly goal.

The sting of frustration cut deeply when I was asked to share my room with another boy just arrived from a town on the opposite side of my native hills.

He came to Ascoli to go to school because his father had money.

He came to do what I could not wish for.

The boy's dialect and manners were different from mine, and I lost no time in ridiculing him.

The landlady joined my laughter at the sight of Giusé trying to wash his face while standing fully dressed, with a scarf around his neck, to avoid overexposure to the chilly water.

We had a toilet, but the only sink was in the kitchen.

Even the toilet posed a problem for Giusé.

Once I found him perched precariously on top of the toilet bowl,

in the manner one crouches in open country.

What I saw in him was a nightmarish caricature of what might have been my own image, as seen by another.

Driven by a mind with no reverse gear, I found myself on a dead-end road that would have me stop too soon in the course of my life.

I would have suffered much less had I understood that life's forward course was not a straight line but included curves and

U-turns.

As it was, I reasoned just enough to trap my thoughts between two negatives:

staying in Ascoli had become a dead-end;

going back to Pretare had all the appearance of failure.

To spare my parents from undue financial burden, I chose retreat to Pretare

without a redeeming explanation.

I rented a bicycle and pedaled up to the City Fortress to look down at Ascoli from a vantage point, to restore my perspective and, in a way, say goodbye to a city that had taught me much— perhaps too much, and too fast.

On the way down from the Fortress I missed a curve and demolished the bike. I only bruised my arms and legs, but the accident was ominous in the way it paralleled my current state of mind.

I went to the Pinacoteca to look at paintings, but spent most of the time looking at a sleeping shepherd carved in marble.

I marveled at the skill required to tie his boots with rigid laces.

I relaxed at the thought of reclining my own body on some high pasture near Pretare.

Mamma was glad to have me back home and didn't really care to know why I had returned.

She had no idea of my inner torments and could not have understood how a healthy body could harbor pain.

I resumed carrying wood and water for the house but what I gained in physical release of my pent-up hurt, I lost in my new awareness of the lower status my work implied.

I made up in the evening by gathering friends at home for my story-telling sessions of what I had seen and learned in the city.

My description of Tarzan's jungle was detailed and lasted longer than the original movie.

Having soon regained a leading position among my own peers,

I started feeling like a man who, after failing to clear a hurdle, walks back to the starting place to have a better run before the next leap.

Greeting everyone and everything on the way, I climbed the hills as a returning baron inspecting his real estate.

Spiked boots on gravel announced my coming to partridges and quails, flying noisily for new cover, not knowing I hunted bigger game.

When I reached the quiet of the pasture, I knew my soul had regained its footing.

Leaning forward against the wind, my body started to run and grow lighter on my feet.

Then the wind held its breath and I fell flat on a mattress of grass.

There I stayed until I saw the fog rolling toward me from knoll to knoll.

I ran before the unfurling, white quilted avalanche that grew taller as it neared me.

I ran until my view became gray all around and I sensed

I had been reclaimed by the mountain spirits.

At fifteen years of age I was outgrowing home, my secure nest.
Steadying my footing on the ledge of a major decision,
like an eaglet, I exercised my spiritual wings for the inevitable flight.
My private hurt for having retreated from Ascoli had now become
determination
to catapult myself from a feeling of shame to a redeeming act of courage.
I was ready to leave my home and family, my friends and
the security of Monte Vettore.
I was ready to cross the vast ocean to rediscover America and myself.

≈

II

A New Beginning

The valley was too narrow to keep its people and crop.
The young left home, and most did not come back.
When to cross the ocean was, in a way, to die,
for those departing and those left behind;
when to die was the way to a new life,
I arrived in New York, to be reborn
all child and almost a man.

I didn't arrive or land by way of a lofty ramp.
From the lowest deck of the big ship I was reloaded onto a flat boat, with some other people and
baggage, and brought across more water into a skyless place that seemed too vast to be enclosed
and too crowded to have a way out.
I didn't know that being the son of an American citizen spared me the ordeal reserved for new
arrivals at Ellis Island.
When the stub-nosed boat came flush with the new place,
I wasn't sure whether I was stepping on land or on the deck of another floating city.
Everything around was out of place: railroad cars and restaurants, people of different stamps
uttering strange sounds that obviously made sense to them.
On this place I was delivered, to wait for someone to tell me what to do next.

Hunger made me bold enough to explore beyond the railroad cars.
My finger, pointing to this and that, was all the English I spoke.
I managed to do with less, rather than suffer the indignity of appearing awkward.
Having learned at home to "Never show your weakness to strangers," I let my eyes speak
determination and defiance as I walked among the natives, on crowded sidewalks,
with my private fears and ignorance;
with my private knowledge from the mountains.

I pointed at bread, under a glass counter, and a woman gave me the whole loaf.
I really wanted a sandwich but thought better than to point at a whole ham.
I put a fistful of change on the counter, then picked up what the lady had not taken.
I saw a man with a cart full of bananas, a fruit I had only seen in pictures, and watched how
other people selected and paid for their purchase. I did likewise and paid with a large enough
coin that would spare me from conceding I didn't understand the asking price, or the change
owed me.
With the novel fruit in my arms, I sneaked behind some freight cars,
with that kind of apprehension Adam and Eve must have felt when they succumbed to the lure
of the forbidden fruit.
My first bite filled the mouth with a tasteless slime.
The spitting and the tossing of the bananas was one reflex.

With an address tag pinned to my jacket, I was forwarded to Akron, Ohio.

There, Italians in a ghetto were bound together by the poverty of the great depression and by a common heritage.

From all along the Mediterranean boot, each brought his peculiar dialect that, out of need and mutual respect, they fused into a new language that resembled nothing spoken on either side of the ocean.

Germans and Poles, as good neighbors, contributed a few words and borrowed as many to exchange greetings in another's language. Here, children of transplanted cultures learned English as a second language and let their young roots take hold on a new land.

America was too vast and too new a country to have a unified personality, in spite of its popular use of the radio.

New York City, with its tall buildings, was all that America was supposed to be to a new arrival, but once the train left the great city, the rest of the country still seemed to belong to the Indians.

So much open space, with endless forests and rivers, was mostly uninhabited except for an occasional shabby hut along the railroad tracks.

I pretended to look for "Red Skins" paddling their canoes or lurking behind trees.

I saw instead African faces—the first I had seen in my life.

I was convinced and glad I had come to a primitive land that promised opportunities to build and explore. It was partial consolation for having been too young to join the Italian troops in Ethiopia.

After two years of waiting, Father had been rehired by the Firestone Rubber Co. and could not meet me at the train when I arrived.

I walked up and down the station looking for someone I might recognize from pictures of relatives I had seen at home.

I listened for someone using my language while I walked away from a young lady who insisted on chasing me. I glanced at a card she flashed before my eyes, and there I saw my name.

I realized then that someone had been charged with putting me on the right train and picking me up on arrival—a bit of information I would have appreciated when I thought I was alone in a big world. Smiles of mutual relief is all I shared with my welcoming party, whom I didn't totally trust until her car arrived at a home on Lane Street, with the confirming No. 928.

I soon realized why Americans washed so often.

Everything I touched left black smudges on hands and clothes.

Akron was the rubber capital of the world.

The smoke and smell that saturated the air and coated buildings with a uniform gray was a small price for the opportunity to work.

People came to America to earn a living and save enough money to retire in a cleaner part of the planet, usually their native land.

Akron smelled like the kitchen of the world, a necessary place in the human household, where basic tasks are performed to benefit the family of man.

Shocked to find Americans living in wooden houses, my thoughts turned toward my distant home, as a child turns to his mother when confronted with a sudden change.

The world of Pretare and Ascoli was the one I knew. My birthplace was to me a source of reference of stone buildings and durable monuments.

Rome I knew as ancient history, illustrated with evidence of the "Eternal."

Naples I saw in passing on my way to the boat and its bright, marble buildings were the last to fade from sight when I entered the limbo of water.

From what I knew of the world and its history, civilized people built their homes with permanent materials.

Only Ethiopians live in wooden shacks, Mussolini told us.

～

My cousin Ned
Arrived years ahead.
He spoke like a native
And did the talking for me.
"Straight from the old country!"
He said, pulling at my shoulder
With a side embrace, as one
Showing some new specimen.
I heard only jungle sounds
From people that otherwise
Looked normal.
What I said,
I said with my eyes.

I tried to walk alone
And stumbled on a stare
Aimed from two steps ahead
And three steps on my right.
I stared back,
As one animal to another.
To that he smiled,
And I thought
His smile tilted
Too much on one side.
I struck first,
Then, pulled back
To decide if wrong,
Or right.
He just stood,
And I stood, even.
Lifting both hands,
Shoulder high and
Palms facing out,
I signified peace, but
Not quite surrender,
Then walked away
Looking over my shoulder
Until he too departed,
Perhaps thinking
"A deaf and dumb!
The poor bastard!"

Dati e connotati del Titolare (1)

Professione *lavoratore*

figlio di *Giovanni*

e di *Angelini Letizia*

nato ad *Arquata Tronto*

il *7 maggio 1921*

domiciliato ad *Arquata Tronto*

Prov. di ASCOLI PICENO

statura *1.51*

occhi *castani*

capelli *castani*

barba ___

baffi ___

colorito *naturale*

segni particolari ___

(1) Colonna riservata ai connotati della moglie

Figli

Nome	Data di nascita	Visto

Fotografie (1)

(1) Spazio riservato alla fotografia della mòglie

Firma del Titolare

Antonio Caponi

(2)

Autentificazione della firma *Di Caponi Antonio*

Firma dell'Autorità *Il Commissario Prefettizio*

Dato *23 Luglio 1936 - XIV*

(2) Firma della moglie

CAPONI,
SURNAME

Antonio,
GIVEN NAME

Italy,   May 7, 1921.
COUNTRY OF BIRTH   DATE OF BIRTH

Italian,   brown
NATIONALITY   COLOR OF EYES

PORT OF ARRIVAL   STEAMSHIP

DATE ADMITTED   STATUS OF ADMISSION

IMMIGRANT'S SIGNATURE

ORIGINAL.   IMMIGRANT INSPECTOR

Father and Uncle Rocco boarded at their sister's home.

I was the latest addition to a household that also included Uncle Sam and my three cousins.

Aunt Tomassina was the only woman in the house.

She cooked, washed and mended clothes.

She canned tomatoes and peppers; scrounged and rationed our food.

Uncle Sam made wine, once a year, while Aunt Tomassina mixed "moonshine" with assorted flavors to make Italian *liquori*.

Cousin Ned and I picked up the illegal spirits from another family.

We carried gallons of the basic stuff to make amaretto, anisetta and other festive drinks for women and children to sip, while the men drank wine and talked of better times.

Smoking a pipe or looking through a glass of wine bolstered the men's wisdom and their insistence on sharing it.

At the usual after-dinner sessions, Uncle Sam prevailed in most arguments.

An eye defect helped in making his expression impenetrable.

With his good eye he would stare down one person while the other eye, bulging almost out of its socket, rotated in all directions, blindly but intimidatingly.

Uncle Sam was foreman of a gang of ditch diggers.

He knew his way around people of all nationalities.

To me he said, "When people talk to you and you don't understand, answer 'no fruste'."

I had no way of knowing that those words were alien to the English language.

When foreigners worked with other foreigners, all unknown words were assumed to be American.

On matters of honor I was told, "If anyone calls you 'wop' or 'dago', punch him in the face."

When I asked what the words meant, they looked at each other and shrugged their shoulders.

Uncle Rocco was a shoemaker who had never made a pair of shoes.

"In this country everything is factory made," he explained, as if in answer to my thoughts.

We both knew that in our native town all basic things were locally made, at a pace that hands and mind could follow—as naturally as Nonna spun her spindle to roll the flax that made the thread that made the linen that made our sheets and pillow cases.

Every child knew how his shoes were made—on the lap of a proud artisan who manually worked the leather and proudly held a shoe at arm's length to look and savor the results of his labor, while humming in approval.

"In hard times, mending shoes is good business," Uncle Rocco bragged above the noise of several machines running idle as he spoke.

The scratchy sound of loose belts mingled with the hum of buffing wheels that urged the flesh and nagged the mind with the "Hurry, hurry!" reminder to keep pace with the machines.

ROCCO'S SHOE REPAIRS was brushed in bold strokes on the entry door and on the front windows, on the side walls and on a standing sign that tripped pedestrians not particularly responsive to the cluttering business of soliciting business.

A display counter divided the full length of the shop.

On one side, a small man operated the impressive machines that cut leather and stitched soles, trimmed high heels to a fine point, and buffed a new life on old shoes.

On the other side of the counter, customers sat to read their paper or hide their face behind it, while for a nickel, a young assistant shined their shoes.

The thrifty clients remained standing to look at pictures on the wall: Italian peasants in their regional costumes, panoramas of Florence, Venice and other important places most Italians had never visited.

Old enough to be a confirmed Italian,
and young enough to become an American,
I compared the right and wrong of a previous life
with the right and wrong of the new one.
I learned as an infant learns, without the aid of speech.
I learned as a man learns, when he has something with which to compare.
I learned that shaking hands is not an arbitrary convention.
Reassurance and understanding is conveyed skin to skin,
to span the gap between language and meaning;
to make binding what words may have tentatively agreed.
I learned that some rights and wrongs are basic to survival,
while others are valid as per agreement.

No teacher spoke my language. No book in school translated it.
Only the numbers in the arithmetic book were familiar.
I checked the answer in the back pages and compared those numbers with the
numbers in the question, to deduce what might be the problem I was to solve.
From my efforts, the sixth grade teacher concluded,
"He really reads English. He should try harder to give it voice."
In the afternoon I sat with first graders.
I squeezed my 15 year old body in a miniature desk where my teacher,
out of despair more than hope, placed a picture book for me to color.
I watched for the assent of nodding heads and heeded the giggles of toothless children
to determine what color was right;
then, I used *giallo* next to the word yellow
and pressed *nero* next to black.

Akron, Ohio, 16 Ottobre 1936
That much is straight.
The rest is translation:
"Today I held a boy on the ground..."
But, wait; the story is old!
I should say, in telling.
"... a boy held a boy..."
And the first boy, I think,
I should not still call "I".
True! He had my name, and loved
The mother I love today, but
Who is to say, after many years,
That he and I are related,
Or that he even resembles "I?"
As it is:
It was a boy who held the other down,
It was he who kept the diary,
With all the "me" and "mine"
Now imprinted in the deeper folds
Of what I still call "I."
As it was:
It was my knee on his belly;
His throat in my hand;
The other I held cocked
Over his face.

The rest,
Cousin Ned should tell.
He stopped the fight,
To explain the local rules,
While his head reprimanded
From side to side.

~

Lacking words, I resorted to silent methods of gaining notice from my peers.

I could draw and I could fight.

Both skills helped to relieve my frustration with being singled out as a "foreigner."

My art teacher gave me paint and paper to use at home, convinced that all Italians are born artists.

I was glad to please her by doing something I had always done to please myself.

The history teacher went too far. She made me stand in front of class to read aloud words I could not pronounce or understand.

She put an arm across my shoulders, as if to make clear there was no malice in her torturing me.

I wiped my brow and shook my shoulders to dislodge the touch of my tormentor.

I paused to peer over the book, to make eye contact with every boy in class to remind them of the consequences of not suppressing their urge to giggle.

Perkin's Park had recreational facilities for people of all ages: students, dropouts and unemployed adults.

In a wooded area of the park, two trees served as corners of an unmarked ring.

Boxing gloves hung from a nail on each tree.

Daily, I put on a pair of gloves and waited in my corner for any comer that would put on the other pair.

I fought the first to win the right to fight the next.

My advantage was strength, compressed and concealed in a small body.

The humiliation of finding most Americans my age taller and heavier than I was the extra incentive for challenging bigger men.

Those who accepted my unspoken challenge were mostly Negroes, equally frustrated by social injustices and inspired by due admiration for the popular boxing champion, Joe Louis.

One of the onlookers went home to tell his sister about "a tough kid, just arrived from Italy."

Yolanda told me years later, how early she decided to be my wife.

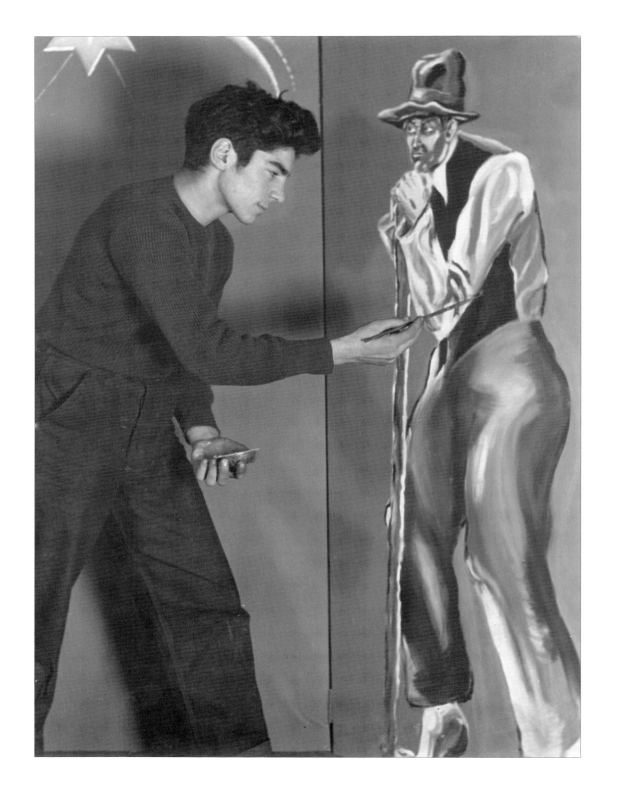

For my social life, I tagged along with cousin Ned.

One time, he took me to the house of the "nicest girl in town."

Her parents welcomed us in Italian, then retired toward the kitchen.

Their daughter Yolanda sat on the sofa with Ned.

I sat on another chair across the living room.

Ned talked and talked, while I looked at a comic book and tried to match words with the pictures. He talked and talked while Yolanda looked in my direction and I pretended not to look back.

For the first time, I was glad of my forced silence.

My shortcoming caused me to appear poised and mysterious,

while my eloquent cousin dissipated fantasy and romance in hot air.

When the mother of the house brought coffee for her young guests, Yolanda handed me a cup.

I reached with both hands. I reached toward her fingers.

She smiled, and we paused, to prolong our touch.

With no sister and no women among the young relatives,

my knowledge of girls was mostly gossip and fantasy.

In Ascoli, I knew where the Bordello was and even my landlady knew where to send her husband, as a parting suggestion, at the end of a domestic argument; but, at sixteen, I still didn't know the word "sex" in any language.

At a younger age, what I knew as a special feeling, Mamma called "sin."

The priest, at confession, sanctified Mamma's opinion by asking me to do penance with seven Padre Nostri and seven Ave Marie.

Cousin Elio, who was my age and attended high school while I learned English in sixth grade, was no more enlightened than I.

He told me about the strange behavior of a girl who asked him to kiss her.

Laughing off his frustration Elio admitted, "I couldn't do it! Every time I puckered my lips, she opened her mouth."

Necessity made of me an observer.

From what others could tell, I was deaf and dumb;

but before I learned to speak I understood.

Girls told me things they normally told a mirror,

and I didn't let on, not even with a nod.

Unencumbered by words, I responded eye to eye

and together we blushed with the pleasure of knowing.

In anticipation of Mamma and brothers joining us in America,

Father and I moved to a larger house with another Italian family.

There I used the attic to sleep and to paint with the oils the art teacher had given me.

The lady of the house visited my room and offered to pose.

She lifted her dress and invited me to compare her fleshy thighs with the idealized

shapes I painted.

Wiggling her hips she backed away from me and I followed out of curiosity and dare.

When I got close to her, she fell limply on my bed and the color left her face.

In panic, I retreated from the room, thinking she had been overcome by a sudden illness

≈

I weep like a wop, for
All the fullish things I say,
While making a fool effort
To convince my tongue
Dat teet don't bite,
In proper English.
"No matter," I'm told,
"From what country you come.
You have a vice to overcome!
You can't go'n stick vowels
On dissa and datta and
Take the H from the oly!"
I try! Even when it's scary
To say aloud
What some words sound like.
I trip on triplets.
Slip over esses
And make cheeks red
Between shirts and sheets.
Butt, what's the use!
Even the O's and U's
Change mode and moods,
To break roots and rules.

~

Within two years of my leaving home, Mamma and my two brothers joined
Father and me in America.
Mamma had abandoned her resolve to live and die in her native land.
She left behind her symbol of pride and status—
the beautiful home that she and her husband had built with love and labor,
with mutual sacrifice of living most of their married life away from each other.
She left behind the living and the dead, the security of a predictable future.
She chose uncertainty, in an alien world, to reunite her family under one roof.
It was a small roof, covering a lesser home in a humble neighborhood that sheltered
our reunited family in America.
It was a time of national austerity and hope.
It was a good time for sharing a new beginning with a new people.

Mamma remained the loving parent I had known as a child.
Her love never faltered, even as she became one of that special kind of people who
left their roots in another land like cut flowers, soaking in stagnant water,
living their life through rootless stems.
This description also fit my father and many of our neighbors.
It fit Aunt Tomassina who had brought my young cousins to this country, ten years earlier.
This was a community of laborers who, after months of unemployment, now worked for the
WPA at minimal wages.
Working people did not suffer great shock from economic reverses.
When their fortune stumbled, it didn't have far to fall.
They were close to the ground and grew from it their daily food on unclaimed open land.
They raised their hopes and expectations for their children,
to achieve the dream that eluded them in this "land of opportunity."

≈

That everything is "relative" is one of the first things I learned in the new world, and that I learned long before I knew the word.

The American economic depression was to me a time of plenty.

Not that I felt poor when I had even less.

The Depression was a fun time, when people balanced material scarcity with an abundance of human resources.

It was a time when the old and the young gathered as families, and families gathered in each other's homes, each bringing something to share: food and wine for the table, stories to stir sentiments and laughter, an accordion to play and by which to dance.

It was a time when the American "Melting Pot" contained a variety of flavors, and the street-language included a smattering of German, Polish and Italian.

This informal background, that often retarded correct use of English, did not impair communication or understanding.

Strong family bonds and neighborly interaction among diverse cultures gave understanding a global vision and made of humanity an intimate experience.

I wish I could have asked:
¿Why, you think it wrong,
For a boy to resist saying
"Girl" with a gargle?
¿Why, when you speak,
Your teeth rebel
And bite your tongue and
Your mouth spits
In self-reference?
I wish I could have told teacher
Not to roll her T's in spaghetti
Like one rolls macaroni, and
Not to choke on the capital
of Vespucci's "A"merica!
A sudden laugh
Might have cleared the voice box
Of swallowed words and pride,
And made it easier to swap
"Bacio" for a kiss,
And feel love with "amore."

≈

Love and loyalty are virtues with strong opinions:
Miss Sullivan decided I was a faultless boy.
Whenever I fought, she punished the other student.
When my actions were indefensible, she vouched for my good intentions.
She had been my first grade teacher and, as the new principal,
moved me from the sixth to the eighth grade.
Most of the time she had me paint murals by her office.
In literature class she instructed the teacher to accept my drawings in lieu of written reports.
It was only fair, for a foreigner who understood much better than he could talk!
Besides, I deserved some credit for having taught Miss Sullivan
more Italian than she had taught me English.

When entering high school, at seventeen, I was four years behind my age group;
but really, I was three years ahead, and gaining on a dream to which I had no right
when I graduated from fifth grade in my native country.
Emilio, my oldest cousin, had come of age at the wrong time and,
like many others, opted to quit school to earn a living.
Emilio was a musician of reputed talent.
He took music lessons on several instruments, but
music and art are the cultural outcrops of an affluent society.
Without a supportive audience, Emilio's artistic spirit lacked the energy to go the extra mile.
Late as it was, I decided to sow the seeds of life's gifts in the fertile fields of education,
where the planting season is long, where the harvest is an endless occupation.

South High School was progressive enough to have two art teachers and a wrestling team
to boost my interest.
There I chose courses that required the least speaking in class.
Though my appearance did not betray my age or composure, my use of English made me
conspicuously disruptive.
It was hard for students not to laugh at my asking the teacher for a "shit of paper."
It was harder for me to tolerate ridicule.
I might have learned more on the street, but people who liked me also liked my way of saying
things and made no attempt to correct me. I didn't hear myself as others did, but I
wished the language had fewer gagging sounds and more vowels to form words at the lips,
instead of pinching them between tongue and teeth.

After a period of warming up with soap sculptures, Miss Riblet gave each student a block
of wood that was supposed to keep class busy the rest of the semester.
I took mine home, thinking she wanted it back the next day, as we had done with soap.
I carved my horse with knife and chisel while worrying about the art teacher being too
demanding.
With work in hand almost finished, I approached her desk the next day to find out if I had
understood right. Her comment was a frown of critical surprise
and a request that I follow her to the wood shop.
There, she asked the man in charge to laminate a large block of wood that would keep me
busy the rest of the term.
With almost a smile on her face, the teacher returned to her desk to look at art magazines.
I sanded my wooden horse and meditated on my mistake.

Painting was Miss Glover's specialty.

Competing with the other half of the art department was her daily preoccupation.

She gave me expensive paper and special brushes and made it clear there was more
if I stayed in her class.

I was allowed to sketch in study hall and bring models to class.

The more Miss Glover complimented my work, the more I repeated myself.

Figure drawing and portrait painting became my obsession.

People, more than art, was my passion.

Capturing a person's likeness provoked a primitive sense of power over the painted subject.

There was something very intimate in tracing the outlines of a girl's lips, modeling her
cheeks and rendering her hidden shapes.

What the teacher called art was, to me, a collection of beautiful souls I could take home.

My European reverence for teachers came to an end
when I discovered they didn't know everything.

Neither of the art teachers knew the process of casting
my clay sculpture into a more durable material.

Miss Riblet tried to save face by inventing a solution
that resulted in the total loss of my work.

I went home to cry, and Mamma cried with me.

Mamma had become a spiritual partner in my efforts to become an artist.

What the teacher had done was worse than if the Pope had lied.

At the public library, I found a book on casting, with enough illustrations
to assist my reading.

Alone, in the basement, I worked for days until I had learned
what the teachers should have known.

At a time when teachers were viewed as uncommon people,

our school principal was nearly a god.

In convocations he spoke on moral issues and civic duties as a special kind of patriotism.

Mr. Bryant was really in charge! He visited classes, unannounced, and sat in the back row,

while teachers and students squirmed.

I had nothing to fear.

I had painted his portrait while he sat behind his desk, saying he had seen me wrestle and that he too had wrestled in his youth.

He was no threat to me. I had his soul stacked away at home.

I walked in his office, clutching a plaster sculpture, and explained to the principal where I had been the last two weeks.

He walked me back to the art room and asked me to explain how to make a plaster mold. I spoke while staring at both teachers and, for the first time, I didn't worry about my foreign accent.

Miss Riblet had connections.

She arranged for me to be a guest member of a small club of professional artists who met once a week to draw and paint. "Remember," she said, "these are important people.

Don't rush into your work, as you do in school."

After meeting my sponsors, I took my place behind one

of the swivel boards arranged around a low pedestal.

A robed model came in and took her place.

I looked down at my paper, pretending to retack it on the board.

When I looked up, I saw a naked blond—the first nude woman I had ever seen.

Miss Riblet had not warned me about this development!

Trying to act professionally, I proceeded to study the model the way Miss Riblet might have expected me to do. When I finally shook my head, I saw that my sophisticated colleagues already had the tall figure on paper.

Once I got going, the model lost its importance to what I was doing.

People still say, "An artist works because he is sensitive to beauty," but I knew, even then, that beauty requires no intervention.

It was ugliness and frustration that energized my hands to strip the mossy paint off our modest home, rebuild the wall along the sidewalk and pave the driveway with discarded bricks.

It was the promise of beauty and pride that made me experiment with methods and skills I had not used before. I laid blocks and cast concrete steps, plastered walls and hung new paper.

Once the place looked nice, I didn't make a habit of fixing things.

I was glad to relax on the porch swing and watch people look in my direction,

toward a home that showed care.

Sitting on the porch was the American way of socializing with neighbors and greeting strangers, between the privacy of home and the public sidewalk, where children played hop-scotch and rode their wagons, with one leg on and pushing with the other.

Who could have guessed the porches would become enclosed or omitted altogether or that people would quit using sidewalks!

Before the family car shifted the main entrance from the front to the side, before the front windows were moved to the rear, to look into a fenced-in yard, people liked people and neighbors trusted neighbors.

Individual honesty and neighborly trust was the most impressive discovery I made in America, where children played on streets and sidewalks, left their scooters and balls overnight and found them there the next morning.

Homes did not lean on each other, as they did in the old country, but they were close enough for our family to hear the first cry of each baby born next door.

That alone made us close relatives with our neighbors.

Mrs. Louis, "the Syrian lady," spoke just enough English to make her comfortable with Mamma who had mastered even less of the new language. The Louis' daughters shared our home, doubling as our sisters and playing daughters to Mamma.

The only discord between our two families involved the decorative bricks, outlining our lot, with the sharp corner facing up.

Mr. Louis threatened to remove the dangerous obstacles that tripped his children on their way to our home.

Mamma prevailed by saying in Italian, and then translating,

"Nobody touches what my Tony made!"

Our other neighbors were a recently married couple who lived the private life of honeymooners.

The first day we moved in, Mrs. Adams brought us flowers.

She used sign language to convince Mamma they were not for sale.

She was a beautiful woman, too shy to notice she made me blush.

Mr. Adams was a research worker for the Goodrich Rubber Company. Having taken notice of my interest in sculpture, he brought me samples of an experimental rubber that melted at a temperature low enough to use at home.

Years before the new rubber was available commercially, I used KOROGEL to make reusable molds, to cast plaster sculptures that my brother Damiano sold, door to door.

The smelly smoke, coming from our basement windows, never provoked a complaint from our neighbors.

American women were aggressive and fun, but they weren't for real.
They didn't have the qualities that inspired my people to say,
"What a nice girl!"
There were some suitable Italian girls, but they could only be seen in the presence
of their parents.
A boy could not get too close without entering a marriage agreement.
Going steady was not an Italian thing to do.
That was good enough for me, until it became a matter of pride.
Aunt Tomassina had made up her mind to have one of her three sons marry Yolanda.
When someone suggested I might be a contender for the same girl, cousin Ned replied,
"May the best man win!"
Those words committed me to an irreversible course in life.

Even Italian girls had ways of getting around their parents.
They would go out with one or more trusted girlfriends, depending on
how many boys they were to meet.
Using this thin cover, I took Yolanda to the movies on weekends;
and after she went home, I went to her house to see her again.
One Sunday, her mother opened the door and welcomed me in,
almost too politely.
I knew she had found out.
I heard Yolanda crying her denials to her father in another room.
When he confronted me, I felt shame for even considering lying, out of fear of another man.
Having told him the truth, he asked his daughter to sit on a chair, facing me.
After hearing her confession of love, he turned to me and said,
"You come back when she has finished school."
That is how it happened that I found myself engaged.

∾

While I was becoming an American, Hitler and Mussolini became war allies.
The Germans conquered Poland and France.
To my dismay, the Italians could hardly beat little Albania or the ballet-skirted Greeks.
The radio and daily papers reported German advances and praised their new
blitzkrieg tactics, as they would report a super sporting event.
Nations chose sides in the expanding world arena,
while the Americans debated which side to applaud.
From the sidelines,
most people of European descent rooted for their own,
as any sports fan would root for his home team.

"What you know, Joe!" the title of a popular song was used to make fun of Joseph Stalin's
plight, when the Germans attacked Russia. Political cartoons animated anti-Soviet editorials
in American newspapers.
Sentiments suddenly turned around when President Roosevelt decided, for the nation,
what role our country should play in the world.
Our "free press" changed its tune.
Political views of free-thinking Americans became as regimented as
anything I had known under Fascism.
Even before the "dirty Japs" attacked Pearl Harbor, I was caught in a cross fire of
conflicting loyalties.
I reasoned: wherever my family is, that is my home and country.
What I reasoned, I hoped my heart would follow.

Roosevelt orchestrated domestic needs and world unrest to send the American people back to the factories.

More cars and more radios became available, and even our home added a phone.

I, too, joined the work force while finishing high school at night.

My world was changing fast, and I with it.

What in Ascoli had been a rare privilege of the elite was now within my reach.

I worked to buy my own car.

I worked at the bottom of a deep trench, cutting stone with a jackhammer, because it paid more than a safer job.

Because I could control the lighter tools to refine other people's work, I had charge of keeping the carved wall plumb.

Cutting stone with heavy tools was to become an important link between the rocky mountains of my early life and the carving of my future.

To be able to labor, without risking self-respect or the opportunity to try other things, was a most precious discovery in my new life.

This new experience gave me as much sense of equality and freedom as I would ever need.

I didn't envy the rich people in Akron's West Hill.

I didn't pity the people living in shacks under the North Hill Bridge.

No human condition needed be permanent in the land of Lincoln, where a poor laborer could hope to be president.

As for freedom, it was not an American invention.

Freedom, even under Mussolini, was not something the Pretaresi asked to be given.

Freedom was a quality of the mind, cultivated in the security of family.

It was an inseparable ingredient of being that no government could give or deny.

It was more than language that made of me a foreigner.

I did not share my peers' special kinship with "underdogs."

Strength and health, skills and resourcefulness described my heroes.

Aside from mandatory respect for official authority and elders,

I believed each man determined his relative place in life, person to person, face to face.

When meeting another man, I instinctively determined which of us would have to step aside if we ever met on a narrow trail.

When the animal pecking order was challenged, a sensitive code of honor required that I fight.

No physical hurt could have been more painful than loss of face.

I would as soon not have had reason to fight, but I fought to win.

I could not understand why heroes and cowboys in the movies would pick up a villain off the floor, just to knock him down again.

It seemed to me, when fighting for life, the American sense of fair play belonged in comic books and movie matinees.

Current world events dictated the course of my life independent of my efforts
to direct my destiny.

Things were happening fast, and I didn't quite know if I was celebrating the finishing of
one thing or the beginning of another.

I finished high school and earned a scholarship to the Cleveland School of Art.

The mechanical drawing I learned in night classes was channeled toward my training to
be a machinist, an occupation that promised a possible way to honorably avoid being
drafted in the army.

I became proficient on the metal lathe, making dyes for bullets.

With a temporary license I took Yolanda for a ride in my new car.

It was between the last light of day and the beginning of darkness when I crashed into
the side of an unlit car.

No one got hurt, but the smash-up, like the smashed bike in Ascoli, marked another ending
and the beginning of another major turn in my life.

On July 14, 1942 I was drafted into the US Army.

No sooner had I learned new principles of behavior than the rules changed again.

America was at war, and I had to readopt values I had discarded.

"This is for real!" said the Drill Sergeant.

"In war, good sports get killed!"

It wasn't until I was inducted in the U.S. Army and met soldiers from other states that I came to know America, its people and language.

It wasn't until World War II, when I was returned to my native country as a uniformed enemy of cousins and friends,

that I learned a few things about the rights and wrongs of the world.

~

III

Between Two Worlds

Man is an adaptable animal, with an adaptable rationality.
He prescribes words, then lets words prescribe his thinking.
He strives for independence, then relinquishes his mind and
conscience to regimented actions.
He substitutes slogans for reason.
"We fight for what's right. God is on our side!"
I have heard the same words on both sides of war,
claiming the same rights on behalf of the same God.

≈

Without leaving the land of the free, I found myself trapped in the fenced confines
of an oppressive system.
I was in the U.S. Army, taking basic training, to learn how to forget my own identity
and become an efficient element of an impersonal machine.
Having had my fill of patriotic slogans since childhood,
I resisted the regimentation of a dehumanizing system
that legally revoked the individual rights of the very people
who were to fight under the banner of democracy.
I resisted the process calculated to neutralize conscience
so that a soldier would not be encumbered by shame and remorse
in his prompt execution of a command.
The price for remaining a feeling person was the measure of extra hurt in experiencing
the realities of war.

I would have preferred to be taught the art of self-defense—to kill when necessary, with the full knowledge of the value of the life I took, and the worth of the life I protected.

But, for me, the Army had other plans.

A sergeant tried to teach me how to patch a wounded soldier.

It must have been easier for the Army to put me in the Medical Corps than put a rifle in the hands of a recent alien from an enemy country.

Nevertheless, I thought, "A soldier without a gun is like a man without his manhood."

I found ways of escaping the unrewarding routines and the ordeal of taking orders.

First, I became the unofficial company barber.

Later, I joined a boxing program meant to entertain soldiers and promote good morale.

Boxing might have saved me from the serious consequences of my reluctance to take orders.

For any humiliation I endured, I had a safe way to vent it.

From basic training at Camp Picket, Virginia, I was transferred to Fort Mead, Maryland, where I continued boxing and wrestling and won the camp championship in the 155 lb. class
in both sports.

Instead of hospital duty, I worked in the motor pool, making use of what I had learned in Ascoli.

After designing the logo for the hospital paper, I was moved to the paint shop to stencil numbers and stars on trucks and jeeps.

During slack time, I painted war pictures.

The Colonel took notice and asked me to paint his wife's portrait.

After a few more requests by other officers, the "Old Man" assured me I could keep on painting for the duration of the war.

That undue protection caused me to apply for a transfer into a more manly service.

Camp Ritchie, Maryland was a deceptive place.

It was more like a summer resort than a Military Intelligence Training Center.

There, a soldier did not "pull KP" or make his bed.

He was either on a field-exercise or in class studying history or geography, interpreting aerial photos or practicing interrogation.

The men at Camp Ritchie were combat soldiers qualified to use a variety of weapons, radio transmitters and the language of the enemy.

Close combat was considered his most practical defense and the best way of killing silently.

I resisted taking turns playing the victim, letting another soldier wrap a piano wire around my neck. I explained that "make believe" could only neutralize my already primed reflexes for self-defense. The instructor agreed, and allowed me to contribute my combined experience in boxing and wrestling, and, most important, the unsporting ways of street fighting.

Dormant conflicts and doubts, convictions and contradictions, kept on bumping heads.

What high purpose or sacred duty was a mortal creature to follow without betraying God and man in the service of a country!

At my first interview for training, I confessed to having been a squad leader of the black-shirted Balilla.

Reassuringly, I was lectured on the difference between the obligatory involvement of the average Italian and the fanatic few elites who hoped to gain by pushing Italy in a war that was becoming disastrous for the Italian people.

It was reasonable and convenient for me to conclude:

I belonged to the simple people who had more relatives in Leominster, Massachusetts than there were souls in Pretare.

The German Panzers in North Africa retreated toward Tunis,

leaving behind their Italian allies to be taken prisoner by the British.

This mass surrender brought a bit of reality to my conditioned image of Italian soldiers.

I began to understand why my countrymen made poor fighters when not fighting for their home.

Mussolini was a romantic braggart who had promised to win the war with his "million bayonets."

Now, his equally romantic troops were stranded on foot, with not much more than their parade bayonets. Defensively, I thought, perhaps the Italian soldier is too human and too much of an individual to keep step in marching formation.

Our class was the last of its kind to finish its training at Camp Ritchie. It was the first class to become obsolete, when General Badoglio and the Allies began plotting an armistice.

Our overtrained group, no longer rating a special flight overseas, would be taking a fast boat headed to Casablanca, then to Algiers, via cattle-train. There we would be reassigned as members of the Allied Military Government of Occupied Territory.

Efforts by the Italians to make peace with the Allied forces had failed.

The Germans had taken over Italy and made of the country a battleground.

∼

It was a gray day, though it was the 14th of July 1943 —exactly one year since I first donned the
U.S. Army uniform.

Gray smoke and fine soot hung low around the train all the way to the port of embarkation
in Newport News, Virginia.

Piling gray on gray, guns and trucks, soldiers and supplies, were loaded on gray boats.

The camouflaged ships blended with the gray of the sea and of the sky.

They blended with the empty gray of loneliness.

Before us was a misty sea, hiding German submarines, daring us to cross, daring me to return the
way I had come, seven years younger.

The home and family I left behind in coming to America, I left behind again, in recrossing the
vast ocean between my two worlds.

"She can outrun any German sub," we were told, as our unescorted ship banked on one side to
make a sharp turn, to perform one of her zig or zag maneuvers to avoid a possible ambush.

On crossing the no-man's ocean, we saw nothing but the edge of the world and the abyss beyond.

The only sign of war was our own presence.

The soldiers were tense, resigned, or sulking in their bunks.

They paced the narrow spaces, or circled the deck, as if their steps could alter either speed or place
of destination.

At night, within the ribbed hull of the ship, thousands of souls huddled as one, as the pregnant,
American vessel floated in the primordial womb of life.

∾

My home, on two continents,
My soul, tossing in mid-ocean,
My body, carried by the tides,
Landed ashore on native soil.
On a ledge between two worlds,
Where plants lose their roots,
Where the sea discards it dead,
I stood on no-man's land
Between my double sorrows
Of leaving and returning.
A son, I departed,
Tripping sideways with each "Addio."
A soldier, I returned,
Transformed and reassembled
Into an army of thousands,
As an interchangeable segment
Of an armored millipede walking on many legs.

≈

A dark horizon connected the sea to the hills of Salerno
As I, but a lump in a cluster of helmets, approached the
Strip of sand that separates invaders from defenders.
"Forward!" My legs obeyed, without a goal to gain.
To the rear was the sea. Ahead was my past.
Either direction was retreat.
The mind formed no words, as visions bombarded the senses:
The horror of my face under an alien helmet,
My people and home in the near mountains.
Love and fear compressed into pain, as the hills ahead
Connected to the hills that connect to the slopes of Monte Vettore,
As the nodules of my brain connect to each other,
Within the vault of my soul.

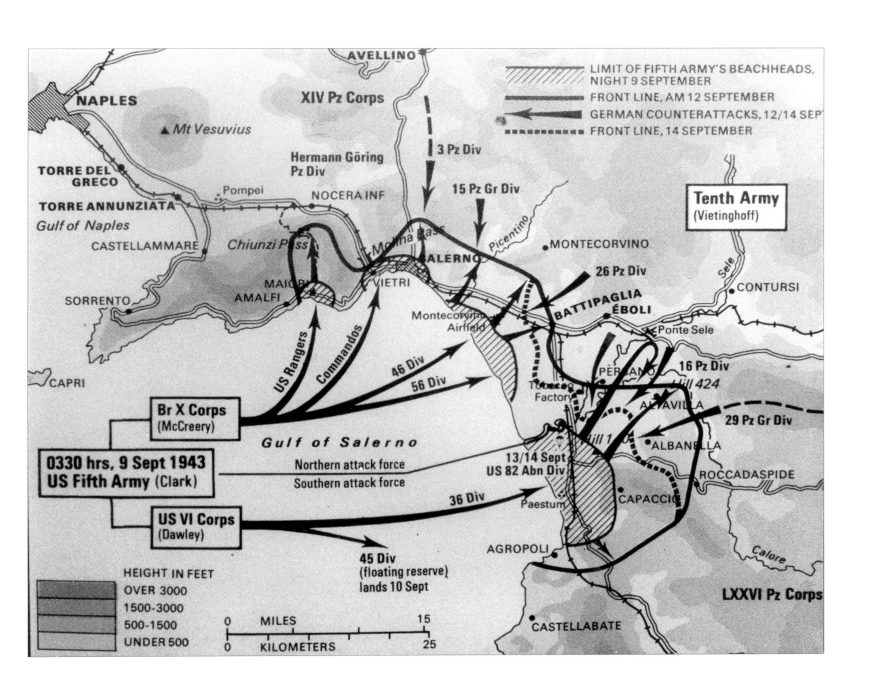

NAPLES

Mt Vesuvius

TORRE DEL GRECO

TORRE ANNUNZIATA

Gulf of Naples

Pompei

CASTELLAMMARE

SORRENTO

CAPRI

AVELLINO

XIV Pz Corps

Hermann Göring Pz Div

NOCERA INF

Chiunzi Pass

MAIORI

AMALFI

VIETRI

Molina Pass

SALERNO

3 Pz Div

15 Pz Gr Div

Picentino

MONTECORVINO

Tenth Army (Vietinghoff)

26 Pz Div

CONTURSI

BATTIPAGLIA

ÉBOLI

Ponte Sele

Sele

Montecorvino Airfield

US Rangers

Commandos

46 Div

56 Div

Tobacco Factory

PERSANO

16 Pz Div

Hill 424

ALTAVILLA

29 Pz Gr Div

Br X Corps (McCreery)

Gulf of Salerno

Northern attack force

ALBANELLA

Hill 1

ROCCADASPIDE

0330 hrs, 9 Sept 1943 US Fifth Army (Clark)

Southern attack force

13/14 Sept US 82 Abn Div

CAPACCIO

US VI Corps (Dawley)

36 Div

Paestum

AGROPOLI

Calore

45 Div (floating reserve) lands 10 Sept

LXXVI Pz Corps

CASTELLABATE

LEGEND:

LIMIT OF FIFTH ARMY'S BEACHHEADS, NIGHT 9 SEPTEMBER

FRONT LINE, AM 12 SEPTEMBER

GERMAN COUNTERATTACKS, 12/14 SEPT

FRONT LINE, 14 SEPTEMBER

HEIGHT IN FEET

OVER 3000

1500-3000

500-1500

UNDER 500

MILES

0   15

KILOMETERS

0   25

An avalanche of flesh and steel rolled uphill, against man and nature.

Soldiers on foot, soldiers on wheeled-armor branched out in deep gullies, on bridgeless roads,

that followed the way of waters, draining from higher slopes against the step of climbers.

Mountains behind mountains, each protected a favored village;

all obstructed the way to Rome.

Soldiers and generals cursed God and his obstacles for favoring the defenders.

I favored the mountains, their lofty serenity, beyond the deeds of man, indestructible and

unperturbed by the flash of cannons.

The mountains in turn favored all creatures.

Their caves were full of homeless civilians, even as soldiers of unlike uniforms scampered

from crevice to crevice, to find safety on their rocky shoulders.

Where two roads crossed, Battipaglia lay razed.

Further on, Eboli partially stood, without a soul in sight.

A *Carabiniere* came out of hiding, to yell *"Americani!"* in welcome.

After a short exchange of smiles we asked him to reveal where the town's people were hiding.

Leading the way for some of us to follow, we reached a cave and entered its darkness.

Not a sound came from within. My flashlight led the way in,

as I called out *"Amici!"* to reassure myself and the dark.

We found old men and women, huddled in a corner,

trying to keep their young girls and children out of sight.

I turned the light upon myself, so they might see, I was one of them.

When I looked again, their eyes were blind with fear,

their ears were deaf to my words.

I was an alien. My uniform confirmed it.

At Avellino, people kept their windows and doors partly open to wave at passing soldiers, with proportioned fear and curiosity.

I waved my greetings in their local dialect, to which a girl responded by pulling at my hand, "Mamma, Mamma, this one speaks Italian!"

I returned to her home, armed with food and apprehension, and found the mamma lady, with her daughter, and four other girls. After supper she took the only candle and asked that we follow to a bedroom where two full-sized beds were pushed together under one quilt.

Afraid to stay and too proud to run, I fumbled with my boots while the girls slid under the great spread to modestly remove their clothes.

The elder woman gave thanks to God, for having sent a protector to her household.

The others joined in chorus to give thanks, with occasional interruptions, to suggest where, in bed, I could best rest my soldier-weary bones.

It seemed scandalous that an American soldier should speak Italian without a foreign accent.

I found it easier to imitate broken Italian than explain my predicament of a dual loyalty.

Besides, I had already learned that people would rather open their heart to a foreigner than tell half a truth to a neighbor.

So, I went on listening to people who told me things they would not have told, had they suspected how well I understood.

They spoke of their loyalty to Mussolini who, for all his faults, had restored their Roman pride after centuries of submission to foreign powers.

They referred to the "Liberators" as a horde of mixed races that destroyed what they conquered.

Women expressed disdain for their own men as any other female in nature disdains a loser.

All that is good and all that is bad was pushed to the extreme, and I, a participant and spectator, learned from this episode of human magnification.

≈

Some people speak of courage as something inborn or, at least, learned.
There is no such thing as raw courage.
The only thing real is fear:
The fear of a mother to lose part of herself,
When she chances death to save her child;
The fear of a man to lose face, when self respect outweighs danger;
The fear of a soldier, conditioned to see his safety in the safety of a fellow soldier.
It is fear that compels a hero to disregard his safety,
to save another, in whom he sees himself.
It is fear, brought in balance by love and human fellowship, that one calls courage;
unless it be confused with insensitive folly.

Monte Vessuvio waved its smoky wave.
Napoli hid its ruins behind the Royal Palace.
And I, for a moment, regained the heart
Of a son at home.
Nothing is more disarming than a suddenness of feelings.
Nothing hurts more than the plunge from normalcy
To the abyss of destruction.
A whole building exploded,
Spewing people and broken marble
All over the crowded square.
I don't remember either courage or fear
As I pulled at limbs protruding from the rubble.
I remember most vividly, picking up a steel helmet
With part of me splattered inside it.
I remember hurting, at the thought of my mother
Receiving the news that I was dead.

Before fleeing Naples, the Germans booby-trapped the main post office.
Unsuspecting civilians came out of their hiding place to reclaim the streets.
Friendly troops gave out chocolates to people of all ages.
Hundreds of American soldiers were bivouacked in the massive building
when its walls exploded all over the Municipal Square.
Nothing heavier than dust fell on my body, but
on touching the warm blood of a dead soldier
I had trouble separating my own identity from that of a fellow GI.

Behind a hill, blocking from view Monte Cassino,
soldiers and civilians shared Venafro as fellow villagers.
Finding a small accordion in the loft of a private home,
I recalled a tune from the attic of my memory.
The Chief of *Carabinieri* came to the house on the run.
He expected to find a demented person or a fanatic Fascist
playing defiantly the theme song of the Black Shirts.
The *Maresciallo* cried *"Pazzo! Pazzo!"* all the way upstairs.
"You will be the death of us all!" he scolded as a warning
to a fellow Italian, with no intention of apprehending him.
When he came face to face with the perpetrator of such a folly,
his embarrassment showed the paleness of fear.
I wish I could have told him that, I too,
had a foot on each side of the right and wrong.

Soldiers and civilians waved at the American fighter plane displaying
the unmistakable white stars.
The P-38 made a last pass toward its own people, like Judas approaching
Jesus for the kiss of death.
A smoke bomb marked Venafro—a liberated town at the base of a hill that
looked too much like Monte Cassino.
No amount of waving and crying prevented the bombers from following their target-spotter.
The Liberators arrived, like silver angels ordained by a partial god to dispense death from high
heaven, with no more cruelty or compassion than if bombing the children of Satan.

Of all the follies of modern war, few were more inane than the destruction of the
St. Benedict's Abbey.
I saw the American winged pride dive from the sky to shame, to drop bombs on
Monte Cassino, just to lower the lofty mountain by the height of its crown.
Frescoed vaults collapsed, exposing Moses and Christ to an open view of devastation.
Then the walls too collapsed, forming a barricade of ancient icons, carved stones and
human bodies.
The Germans who had previously respected the historic sanctuary, were now free to occupy
the ruins that barred the way to Rome for months.

Posters and newspapers on the German side of Italy,
believers and non-believers of Christ or Democracy, cried in alarm,
"The Barbarians are coming from the south."

"Thirsty for blood and booty, the savage African and Asiatic hordes want to bivouac
in the sacred walls of Rome."
This was the image of the Allied Armies presented by the Fascists to the Italian people.
Pamphlets showing unflattering pictures of African and American Negroes, New Zealanders,
Indians and Asians, were distributed under the heading; "These are the Liberators."
Beyond the frightening pictures of colored troops, the new image included "civilized whites"
in pilot uniforms—destroyers of historical monuments.
The bombing of the Abbey at Cassino had reunited Italians and Germans in a common
battle cry:
"Defend Rome. Defend your home and family."

≈

Ecco
i liberatori...

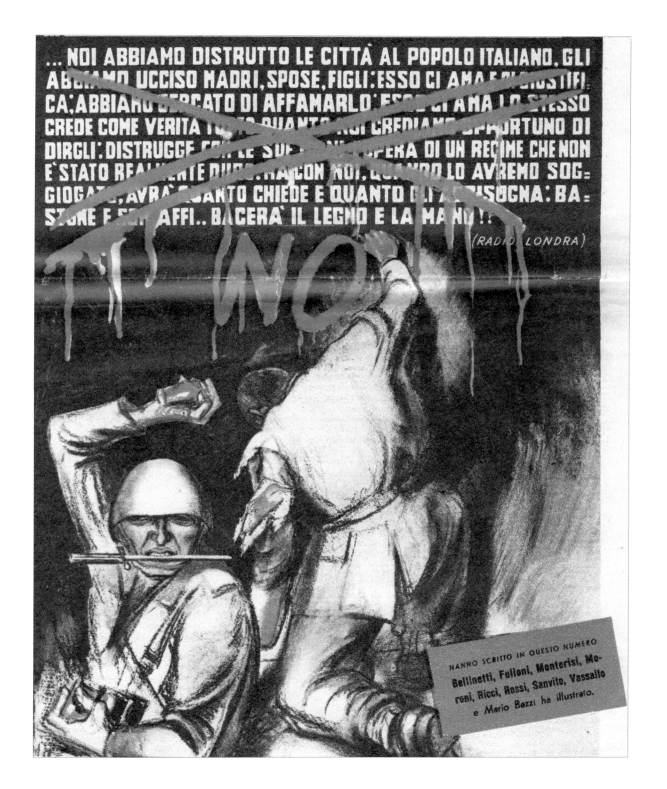

There are things still hiding in the mind: moments of fear, without beginning or ending, hanging on with the wet uniform in a ceaseless rain, unrelated to events, time or places.
A gray mood muddled thinking, like the mist rolling downhill mingled with the rain in a muddy world within a world, experienced a bit at a time, by a mind within the mind, within the short view in a fog.
I recall, not knowing where I was heading to, or coming from, when I crossed the narrow bridge over a swollen stream that threatened to demolish what soldiers were still securing, against the onrush of nature.
Slushing through mud, in an open jeep, I moved toward fear:
fear of going beyond the line of no return,
fear of getting stuck on the wrong side of the stream, if the bridge should wash away.
I tried to reconstruct where I was, but the ruts of memory and the roads of southern Italy would not connect.

The moans of the wounded were not heard
Through the whine of mortar shells.
The brittle blast of metal-spattering bombs
Did not carry beyond the valley.
A heavy sky, dragging its belly across the arena,
Covered the hills and battlegrounds
With its wet winter clouds.

≈

At the request of Major Griffen, a British Military Governor I had known since landing in Italy, I was transferred to the British 10th Corp, at Sparanise. I served as his interpreter at weekly court sessions, as driver and body guard on our visits to the front where civilians of newly liberated towns required instruction and government.

I gave voice to the Major's authority and he, in turn, put in action most of what I knew of the people he governed.

With his encouragement, I explained to the grandfatherly Governor, he shouldn't judge simple Italians by what their words and deeds meant in his own country.

My literal translation of what a man said when accused of stealing food did not convey truth as I knew it.

These were the people who were told, as I was told since childhood,

"When traveling and hungry, what you take of another person's tree or vine is not stealing, unless you take more that what you have eaten."

Where the front stalled, Minturno separated two armies, on opposite sides of its hill and made of the town a no-man's land.

I pushed women and children out of their houses, away from unfinished meals, with no more than they could carry on their body. Herded on the blind side of the hill, the Major pointed them toward the Garigliano Bridge—the way beyond the reach of cannons.

A procession of lamenting souls filed downhill; some pleading to go back in town for something they had forgotten or a relative they had not seen in the crowd.

I looked from face to face, fearful I might see Mamma, or hear her voice among the sobs of bitterness and pain.

I thought of my grandmothers, awaiting the war to pass them; unsuspecting that I might be the one pushing them to safety, even if they saw in me a cruel invader.

Leaving the jeep on our side of the hill, the Major and I inspected the town we couldn't yet claim.
The Germans on the opposite side of the hill made similar visits into Minturno, without seeking
hostile contact.
I stood guard to prevent an accidental encounter, while the Old Man looked at what was left
of a house.
He looked intently at some tea cups left on a shelf, obviously resisting setting a bad example
in front of a young subordinate.
Sure of his thoughts, I stepped in front of him and piled the cups in my helmet, while assuring
the gentle man the cups would not survive the next mortar shell.
The President of the Court nodded his head, while making a small mouth to suppress a smile.

The good Major had the wisdom of age and power of rank.
I had youth, strength and use of the language.
Our fondness for each other grew out of mutual need.
For a British officer, he was more aristocratic than vain,
though his body stooped more from old age than humility.
With grandfatherly thick eyeglasses, he lacked a soldier's bearing but, together,
we enjoyed the best qualities of our combined age and talents.
When the Old Man ventured in towns still contested by the Germans,
he looked at me for reassurance.
As President of the Military Court, the Major nodded encouragement when I, a former peasant,
dared translate the ornate words that puckered the lips of pompous, Italian lawyers.

Driving through Mondragone, I saw an army of little people in a rest camp.

They were the survivors of the bravest unit on the Cassino front—the most decorated soldiers, fighting a useless battle to gain time and practice for our inexperienced, young General.

They were a decimated regiment of American-Japanese who, like me, were there to prove their loyalty to America.

They looked like the "Sneaky Japs" shown to our soldiers in propaganda films, while the audience sang "Kill that Jap."

At least these Americans fought their battle far from their relatives who fought as enemies in the Pacific.

Of all the nationalities involved in the war, only Italian soldiers fought in their own land, on both sides of the front.

For all the noble reasons wars are fought, on the frontlines soldiers protect soldiers, as if all the worthy people in the world were in uniform.

On a battlefield, even a dead German evoked more compassion than a dead civilian.

Refugees crowding military roads were pushed aside as irrelevant to waging war.

The Germans allowed old men, and women of all ages, to pass through their lines, to burden the Allied Armies with useless people.

Clad in black, the color of mourning and respect, the refugees came out of desolate roads and mountain paths, as shadowy souls emerging from the miseries of Purgatory.

Not sure of having reached salvation, they cautiously stared with fear-rounded eyes at the annoyed GIs who waved them away to the rear.

Like John the Baptist standing in midstream, I stood in mid-road
to delouse refugees on their way to safety.
Resigned to submission and shame, they loosened their blouses and undid their pants,
as soldiers dusted their clothes and bodies.
I placed the nozzle of a cardboard cylinder under the nearest skirt and pumped DDT up a
woman's legs until a cloud of white dust settled around her feet.
They arrived in small groups seeking food and refuge.
They left with a halo of dust on their heads, like the blessed walking toward heaven—walking
toward Naples, where vice and typhus were rampant.

Lost in the current flow of history, I, an Italian, watched other Italians limp away from Rome.
I was an American, away from home, standing with parted legs on the Appian Way
to intercept the homeless coming out of no-man's land.
I was a soldier, advancing toward Rome with the Allied Armies, though I felt sure I had gone
that way before.
On the Appian Way, I had marched with the Roman Legions, bringing home war booty and
slaves from conquests in Africa and the Orient.
On the Appian Way and in my thoughts, I marched with fellow Americans and fellow Romans,
with the African and Asian allies, with the current victors of an ever-jousting humanity.

I was on an errand in Naples when German planes raided the city and I followed a group of women scurrying for cover into a private home.

In the darkness of a crowded room, the women made small talk for my benefit.

One lamented, "Nowadays, only a young woman can provide bread for the family!"

I stopped listening when a delicate hand fondled my private parts and gently pulled me to a bedroom. A dim light revealed a budding girl of erotic beauty, eager to unite at our first touch.

She writhed and moaned and gave me full pleasure.

Indulging my ego, as an afterplay, I pressed the young lover to comment on her convulsive display of passion.

She leaned her head on my chest and cried softly, "I pretended pleasure, the way Mamma taught me, but I like to be hugged, up, close to my heart."

Shame and anger stirred my deeper emotions, and for a long time I held a sister in my arms, with a lasting, protective love.

～

The winter stalemate was a time for moving troops to new positions.

Major Griffen and I ended up with the Polish Corp, in the British sector, where an American uniform was an unfamiliar sight.

On my first day at Cantalupo, the Polish MPs picked me up for questioning.

Speaking English with an Italian accent did not help relieve their suspicion of my spying, and I didn't dare speak Italian.

The Poles released me, an American soldier, to a British Major.

The sudden change of expression on the Poles' faces,

from hateful sneers to apologetic comradely smiles, was as fearful as the fear it relieved—

fear, that the fine line distinguishing friend from foe, can so easily shift.

Like an adoptive parent, the Major bent a few rules to spirit me away to the famed British 8th Army operating on the east side of the Apennine Mountains.

And I,

playing the part of a grateful son, tried to adjust to the company of the very soldiers who,

in Africa, had captured Mussolini's troops and now were headed toward my home.

I found myself in a different war, with a different mood.

Driving through Isernia, its people looked away from my jeep with obvious scorn.

Our bombers had razed their city after the Germans had left it whole.

The people of Cantalupo did not sing or mingle with the soldiers, who practiced professional indifference toward the vanquished.

This was a thrifty army with little to share with hungry civilians, and much less to contribute to their black market.

Traveling with Major Griffen from Minturno to Campobasso, gave me a rare view of the many nationalities fighting along the Italian front.

In addition to the Poles, Canadians and New Zealanders, all in British uniform,

the Gurkhas and turbaned Indians fought for the British Empire in anticipation of their own freedom from colonialism.

The American Fifth Army was concentrated in front of Monte Cassino, the strategic stronghold and prestigious prize that enticed the ambitious General Clark to reserve for his troops. Not until after he had sacrificed thousands of American lives did Clark relinquish the honor to others.

The French, the Gurkhas and New Zealanders, each pitted their valor against Monte Cassino and each failed.

It seemed clear that the Allies had chosen the wrong approach to Hitler's Germany.

The multinational armies of the free world could not prevail over the mountains that teamed with mud and ice to barricade the way to Rome.

As if by mutual agreement, the Germans and the Allied Armies seemed content to just hold their respective positions for the duration of winter.

Major Griffen turned aside to blow his nose before saying he had been ordered to return the jeep and me to the American front.

To break the silence that followed, he handed me a copy of a letter of appreciation for my service with him that he had forwarded to headquarters of the Allied Military Government.

I shook his hand without saying a word. After a pause, to realign his composure, he clutched my shoulders at arms length. We looked at each other, and both understood.

His stiff-armed touch would be as close as a British officer could come to a spontaneous embrace. Alone on the road, I missed the company of the Old Soldier; but on arriving at 5th Army Headquarters in Caserta, I felt like a prodigal son who, in a family of thousands, had been missed and brought back home.

～

Looking at the war-landscape from a GI's point of view,
Italy was a roadless country of hills and mud.
As for me, I saw the landscape superimposed on a classroom map that showed
"all roads led to Rome" and all the seas lead to all the roads.
Dangling in the Mediterranean Sea, like a limb
from "the soft belly of Fortress Europe," the Italian peninsula
was an irresistible lure for Churchill and his generals.
But, unlike a shark attacking its prey at the flanks,
the Allied sea-dragon took the bait lengthwise,
the way a crappie takes a minnow by the tail.
The spiked bait of rugged mountains proved hard to swallow
when the ruins of Monte Cassino stuck in the throat for six months.

Under the flags of many nations, the Allies fought as a team,
and all buried their dead at the slopes of Monte Cassino.
The French-Africans and the Poles, both exiled from their country, both eager to redeem their
national honor, combined their valor to push past the vengeful mountain.
The generals, who had been long on coming from the land of Hannibal, dreamed of their tanks
matching the feat of his elephants. It was the foot soldier who broke through the mountains, when
General Clark disobeyed his British commander to be the first to enter the Eternal City with his
American army.
The decisive battle was yet to come,
while I waited in Caserta to be assigned back to the front.

≈

Like a tin-soldier, picked from a toy box, I was paired with a French Canadian officer and
returned to the Aurunci Mountains, where I had served with the British Major.
The French Expeditionary Force now occupied the hilly towns that, for months, had echoed
memories of my Pretare.
There English and Italian, the language of my people, had become whispered laments in the
clamor of African dialects.
Defensively, I regained my spiritual identity—an Italian among Italians, among aliens.
Soldiers populated towns and countryside.
Animals and civilians faded out of sight.
The Spring offensive had started.

≈

In battle, bravery and blood prevailed over justice and pity.

The Moroccans lived off the land, looting towns and slaughtering sheep, their favorite meat.

Their lust for flesh matched the abandon of the Senegalese soldiers who raped women of all ages with the same ferocity they fought the Germans.

The French-Africans were the brave soldiers that breached the Cassino front and forced the Germans to abandon the fortress-mountain before the Poles occupied it.

Victory absolved all sins.

The soldiers moved ahead to pursue enemy and glory.

The homeless were left behind to bury their dead.

War is premeditated killing.

The more devious and unsporting the methods the more worthy of praise.

War is a primitive response to fear and boredom brought to its highest intensity in the ultimate sport—man killing man, each hunter and quarry, each hero and villain.

War is the outer explosion of the universal battle fought within each soul, between the polarized duality of human nature—the saint and killer, the compulsive and rational, the greedy and charitable.

When duty and deeds crowded my conscience, I retreated into the cradle of my childhood innocence. There, a dog was a good dog if he fought wolves like a wolf and could be trusted not to bite his owner.

But, a lamb...!

No one ever called a lamb "good."

A lamb had no choice but to be a harmless animal.

≈

Heavy artillery had been secretly massed on the Allied front for the biggest bombardment of the war to date – May 11, 1944.

Spring's new foliage and a deliberate calm camouflaged weapons and soldiers, ready to avenge months of frustration.

At a single command, midnight exploded with hell's angry fire as the landscape erupted with the simultaneous thunder of a thousand cannons.

The sustained pounding drummed against the sky in disdain of heaven and humanity. I held my head between the palms of my hands to protect the eardrums, to help the mind through its rapid transition from terror to awe and, finally, elation. I was standing on the safe side of hell.

The lightning bolts of explosive steel streaking toward the hills ahead brought to mind no image of victims or devastation.

My soul was saturated with patriotic fervor and totally engulfed in the climatic display of absolute power.

San Andrea was a tattered hornet's nest of roofless buildings.

Senegalese troops occupied the empty ruins, while the fighting continued on the near slopes of the hill-town.

No longer an Italian and not totally American, I became a bystander in a surrealistic dream.

In a devastated town, deserted by civilians and off-limits to Americans, I was alone, among "avenging Ethiopians" invading my native land.

Frenzied Senegalese soldiers prodded prisoners back to town with the muzzle of their guns. With hands clasped upon their heads, ashen-faced Germans stumbled on the rubble-filled streets, as angry black soldiers used their rifle butts to push the prisoners through rampant gauntlets.

Feeling pity for the Germans and a fearful respect for the proud Africans, I kept aside from it all. Like Dante, visiting his own hell, I stood on the edge of fear, unsure of my friends and in doubt of a God whose favor was claimed by each side of a warring humanity.

A lone soldier, seemingly unimpressed by the ongoing war, sat on the protected side of a broken wall to explore a found object.

When I drew near, he lifted his black face, adorned with the raised scars of his tribe.

Though, like other Free-French soldiers, he was armed with American weapons and like me wore an American uniform, it was a tense moment before the African warrior smiled the smile of recognition.

I recognized myself in the savage innocence of a man who sat apart from his peers to think and tinker with a new thing. I smiled back as he handed me a broken victrola—I dared not refuse.

Most civilians had abandoned their villages and dispersed in the hills to wait for the war to pass.
There was no joy, no hint of relief, on the faces of survivors coming out of their hiding places;
no sign of anger, no glare of contempt, aimed at the passing soldiers.
With no home awaiting their return, stranded families stood like zombies, with blank stares
still focusing on visions of terror.

Under cover of near darkness, a woman with two teen-age girls approached our AMG post and said,
pleadingly, "Take my daughters and do with them as you please, but keep the black soldiers away
from them." The girls smiled at my nod, and a reassured mother joined other refugees, huddling
together in the open-air asylum we had provided.
The refugees were mostly women. Their husbands and fathers had gone to war, to fight for the
families they had abandoned.
Like Helen of Troy, women have been the subject of abduction and liberation.
They have been the cause and inspiration of wars that made of men heroes, and
women, the spoils.
The simple villagers, who had expected to welcome the Americans, were terror stricken at the
sight of French soldiers. They knew Mussolini had attacked France when that country was already
defeated by Hitler's armies.
Revenge seemed complete when the French unleashed their African hordes amid the
conquerors of Ethiopia.

≈

The Germans were making an orderly retreat.

Their rearguard units used prepared defenses to resist the Allied advance,

long enough to give their main troops time to retreat with minimal losses.

Nobody knew where the enemy would be waiting.

I certainly had no idea when I tried to enter the town of San Giorgio to put up

proclamations that instructed civilians on AMG rules.

With no soldier in sight I thought the front had moved ahead when I drove my jeep

around a burning truck and a disabled American tank.

Then I heard the unmistakable rapid fire of a German machine pistol.

At the same time I saw a few camouflaged soldiers waving me away,

cursing me and the jeep for having drawn fire upon them.

The Germans must have thought of me as unusually brave or foolish for driving a jeep

ahead of the foot soldier.

I was only too glad to retreat with only a punctured tire.

The town of S. Appollinari had been so heavily shelled that our troops decided to bypass it.

When the Major and I left the main road to check on the town, we were confronted with a clearly

marked warning—ROAD NOT CHECKED FOR MINES.

I looked at the Major and he looked at me, each of us hoping that the other would be first to

suggest a sensible retreat. If either of us had been alone we might have chosen otherwise, but war is

a ritualistic exercise of demonstrating manly courage to others.

Fear, already overloaded with images of blown up trucks along other roads,

now braced itself for the instant that might be our last.

I would have preferred to have a gun aimed at my chest then to die a thousand deaths with each

turn of the wheels. Every second, every inch might be the one that brought the tire over the

invisible button that would blow us apart.

Because we were fully aware of the danger, the decision to go ahead was an act of courage.

Had we acted out of blind bravery we would not have agonized every second of the way.

Castro Dei Volsci, almost untouched by war, became a place of refuge for the people of less fortunate towns.

The overcrowded village also became a lure for the combative soldiers who thought of women as war booty.

Finding two white Algerians in the act of roughing-up a mother and daughter, I intervened.

One soldier turned on me and held his rifle against my belly.

At 23, I was, like them, not past the age of folly, that period of reckless daring,

regarded by some as a biological dysfunction afflicting young males

and considered, by others, to be the stuff that makes good soldiers.

I grabbed the man's rifle and wrestled for it.

The French speaking Major arrived just in time to stop the fight.

He disarmed the intruders and ordered them to leave.

I knew the Canadian officer could not disarm the hurt pride of young soldiers with adrenaline already burning in their blood.

The soldiers left, with challenging glares aimed in my direction.

I followed them, to finish the fight.

In the middle of a crossroad, the Algerians turned to face me.

One rushed forward, grunting something in French while throwing a round-house punch.

That was the last thing he did.

With the vicious intent of a street fighter and the trained timing of a boxer, I crashed my fist on his face with the force of a kicking mule.

I hated the bastard on behalf of the whole US Army, for threatening a GI with an American gun. To inflict maximum damage, I snapped my punches like a whip, to cut the flesh and jar his brain, without pushing his face out of reach.

Not wanting "my man" to fall before his face was a bloody blob, I hit with both hands in rapid fire, even as he slumped on the street.

The other soldier stepped in, waving his open hands between our faces, then knelt beside his friend to revive him.

On seeing the fearful civilians watching the fight from behind their closed windows, I understood the deeper reason for my anger.

≈

At the Major's request, I recruited the closest thing to a priest I could find to say mass in the private chapel of the home the Major and I occupied.

Don Alfonso, a monk of the Benedictine order, whose abbey we had destroyed at Cassino, responded enthusiastically to the opportunity of a good meal and the expectation of gaining favors from the Governor.

The Major let the good monk take his confession and I, out of respect to my superior, could do no less.

I put my trust in God to forgive my act of hypocrisy, rather than offend my devout officer.

In complete intimacy with the Almighty,

I recited my sins in English. Don Alfonso did not understand a word, but in his practical wisdom and good faith, absolved me of my sins, in the name of the "Pater et Filius et Spiritus Sanctum."

The Sunday Mass went beyond mere ritual.

The service included everything but the choir.

Don Alfonso gave an emotional sermon for a congregation of two, counting the Major who understood no Italian.

With arms raised high, the good monk thanked God for having sent the Allied troops to liberate his people.

"You have come as the Archangel with the flaming sword to do battle with Satan."

The people on the streets, out of envy or spite, told me how a few weeks before,

Don Alfonso had thanked God and the Germans for defending Rome with the same Archangel and his flaming sword.

~

Italy was crowded with soldiers from all parts of the world, and I had to remind myself from what country I had come.

I didn't want my years in America to become a mere detour on my way to Rome.

Like any other soul in the space of eternity, I came from the place I was last reborn, where my mother and family awaited my return.

To fortify my thoughts, I requested that I be reassigned to an American officer.

Expecting a change, I plodded along with the French through the mountainous German defenses; while the Americans, on the coastal roads, raced ahead to be first in Rome.

On a dislocated front, in constant movement, I ran an errand for the Major and never saw him again.

I had searched, in vain, for the French Command Post and found, instead, American troops on their way to the capital.

Caught in the spirit of mass jubilation among fellow GIs, I went along to be part of an all-American victory parade.

Roma did not fall, nor was it liberated.

The Germans evacuated, to make it a "Free City."

What belongs to the world, need not be conquered.

Untouched by war, amid opposing armies, Rome was a world within a world and, within its walls, was the Vatican.

Soldiers respectfully removed their side-arms before entering St. Peter's Square.

Uniformed souls, longing for peace and spiritual fellowship, entered the sanctuary as devout pilgrims.

They walked between the open arms of Bernini's colonnades, stretching out in welcome from the shoulders of the basilica.

Soldiers and civilians of diverse religions shared a common bond, each experiencing a private dimension of God.

Buildings and fountains, an Egyptian obelisk and pagan sculptures, shared the square with the saints and the cross.

All, expressions of a humanity seeking to define its creator.

All, revealing a quality of heaven in their artistic beauty.

All, including a quality of God in their unifying harmony, in a world of discord.

≈

Beyond Rome, the war took on a different character.

The Germans had spared the Eternal City, and the Allies, in turn, tried to change their image from conquerors to protectors of Italian culture.

The Allied Military Government became the main instrument for the preservation of historical monuments and works of art.

It was no accident that Major Walker became the Military Governor of Siena.

The French-speaking American officer, and my new mentor, was an admirer of fine arts and knowledgeable of Italian history.

He felt at home among aristocrats and scholars and I, on the sideline, became an attentive pupil.

"I understand you took offense at my eating apart from you," commented my aristocratic officer.

Then, before I could answer, he invited me to sit at his table.

Taking soup from the side of a spoon was not part of my upbringing and, god knows, how many other things I did wrong before the Major began his lecture.

"You will some day be an important artist and keep company with refined people...."

The rest of his words blurred my senses as the blood rushed to light up my cheeks with the color of shame.

The truth burned like a branding iron.

I was an Italian of the mountains, an American of the ghetto.

In Siena, in the cradle of the Renaissance, I resolved to become a better Italian and a cultured American.

As more of Italy became liberated, its liberators became more human, in a country of women and children whose fathers and husbands were either prisoners of war or recruited by the Germans.

Loyal to fellow soldiers and fellow Italians, I reviewed English and local dialects to translate love letters between former enemies.
I interpreted the judgment of military courts, where the victor presided, where democracy and justice echoed the ancient cry, "Might makes right."

The soldiers learned Italian songs and taught, in return, the jitterbug.
The Army worried about morale, when among its men,
the German *Lili Marlene* became popular.
Soldiers were rediscovering in the enemy a fellow man,
caught in a common paradox of humanity.

∼

IV

Reunion

The Germans retreated past Florence,
past my home town, in the British sector;
then, they held their ground on the last hurdle of the Apennines.
During the lull of a stalled front I took a week and a jeep away from the war to visit
the place of my birth.
That island of my life, belonging to no country or time, had not been part of my
soldiering realities.
One part of me would not coexist with the other.
Yet I knew that hurt and contradictions would dissolve in a broader understanding.
The war, too, would become another island
and be part of the archipelago in the ocean of my mind.

Leaving the war behind, I retreated toward home with that light footed feeling I've known when
descending a mountain after a hard climb.
From Salerno, up the long, rocky spine of the Italian peninsula, our armies fought an uphill battle.
Every summit won brought in view another mountain.
The roads between were open targets for the guns aiming down from opposite heights.
This I thought, as the jeep and I faced the empty slits of a disarmed pillbox that had denied us free
passage when we approached from the south.
Driving back to Rome, to where all roads meet, to where the Via Salaria begins and disappears in
the deep crevices of the Apennines, I let my thoughts unwind with the road.
I let myself adjust to the gradual release of pent-up feelings I had so long protected from hurt,
under the impersonal color of my uniform.

Retracing at full speed what had been months of crawling, a condensed life rushed past me, as diary pages slipping freely into a blurry fan from under an impatient thumb.

My thoughts moved at a slower pace, to fill in details and contemplate the composite images engraved in the mind.

The olive groves that had camouflaged soldiers and guns of a matching color, stood empty and still on their scarred trunks. Indifferent to my passing, unresponsive to my sentiments and human concerns, they aimed their limbs to the healing sun.

The same light that brought out the colors of innocent flowers, and, in me, a sense of beauty, accentuated the shadow on the darker side of human nature.

I thought of the footsoldier as a fellow mountaineer, climbing a pathless mountain in a fog.

He had no distant view of his surroundings or of the events affecting his life.

Crawling through mud and smoke screen, he saw an alien country, one rock, one bush at a time, each as obstacles or protection, all as intimate trivia that filled his world of fear and discomfort.

I approached Rome from the north, as the Gauls and the Goths had done in centuries past on their way to sack and devastate the noble city.

I recoiled at the idea of peasants, on the wayside, looking at me as a member of the horde, now concentrated between Livorno and Florence.

Couldn't they see I was one of them, just a country boy, reviewing his history lessons about a world he was just getting to know?

The Rome housed in my memory since third grade was still inhabited by conquering Caesars, bigger and mightier than the heroes in the Bible.

Was I really part of an historic event that moved people through time and places, from awe to arrogance, that I should find myself entering Rome in a one-man triumphal procession?

Along Via Del Corso, civilian cars were reclaiming the street,

though most drivers were military officials.

From my mind set, I was the only civilian driving a jeep, slowly replacing classroom images
with the massive reality of the ancient Pantheon.

Victor Emanuel II sat on his bronze horse looking down at Piazza Venezia, undismayed by
the changing fortunes of the country he had unified.

Looking at a conspicuous balcony, my ears filled with the clamor of frenzied voices I had
heard on radio at an impressionable age.

For a moment, the square filled with black-shirted fanatics yelling their refrain *"Duce! Duce!"*
as the dictator, with folded arms, pivoted from side to side to acknowledge the devotion
of his followers.

When Il Duce thrust forth his chin, to signify he had more to say,

I smiled at my thoughts and moved on.

Where the highest peaks of the Apennines compete for space, the Via Salaria ventures amid
their steep gullies and follows the whims of the draining waters that had a head start on the
Roman engineers in cutting a way to the Adriatic Sea.

Beyond the walled city of Rieti, the mountains push their vertical flanks toward each other,
to form a narrow portal that could have inspired the entrance to Dante's Inferno.

Beyond this point, ancient Romans did not pursue outlaws or the freedom-loving people
who settled on vantage places along the Salaria.

Beyond this point, no modern army loitered while passing in single file, with no side escape.

This tract of land discouraged occupation. It made a natural barrier between the British,
moving north on the east side, and the American 5th Army on the west.

My jeep, loaded with a returning son and spare cans of gas, was the only vehicle on the road.

There is no place called East,
No place of arrival called Last.
Life follows its eternal path, and
death is one of its blind curves.
So I thought,
when I approached the last curve that would bring in view
my beloved Monte Vettore.
When I saw it, I died a little.
I died enough to release my child's spirit,
that part of me that stayed unsoiled through the war.
Thus, my life looped on both ends and came together,
child to child.
Thus, pulsating, my vital fluids rose and crowded the soul's chamber, where reason contracts
and the spirit expands to squeeze out the blissful tears of pain and contentment.

On passing Accumoli, I began the count down of towns remaining between my jeep
and my native aerie.
Tufo was the greatest distance I had walked with Nonno when he came to solicit work
making charcoal.
Pescara stood on the gravel that filtered its waters, draining from one side of Monte Vettore.
The town was noted for its *gazzosa*, a prized refreshment and a popular mix for the wine
children drank with their meals.
Arquata was the communal center to which other towns rendered homage, for no better
reason than its fortress tower dominating the Salaria on two sides, as it curved around a
rocky spur, projecting precariously over the river Tronto.
Finally at Borgo, the Salaria continued toward the sea,
while I turned uphill on a familiar side road.

As the middle ground of familiarity obscures the essential qualities of a great person, so Monte Vettore revealed its stately presence from a distance, then disappeared behind the clutter of lower hills that became even taller as the viewer, at close range, lost his sense of relative proportions.

I knew each fold that kept from view the noble mountain.

I knew the importance of covering the last distance that separated

a dream from the full glory of an intimate view of greatness.

Along the road, two miles from home, I recognized a friend of Mamma's. I wanted to call her name and take her in my arms, but decided otherwise.

I offered her a ride with a practiced, foreign accent.

Her fear changed to a smile when I added, "I am American."

She had only seen British soldiers with their shallow-dish helmets.

Mine looked "too much like the Germans'," she said.

My uniform, and eight years of becoming a man, disallowed any chance of my being recognized as a local fellow.

I couldn't resist the God-given opportunity to play the part of a privileged soul, returning from the dead incognito and powerful. AMG, the well-known symbol to civilians, was plainly stenciled on the windshield of the jeep.

My riding companion used her thumb to cross herself and marveled aloud how no simple stranger could anticipate these blind curves!

Had she been less superstitious, she might have guessed right when I made a sharp turn toward my house, though I blocked the road with my jeep in a supreme bluff of arrogance.

The object of my most ingrained love,

symbol of goodness and security since childhood,

the very personification of all that Pretare meant to me,

blocked my passage to the house.

I gently pushed the noble lady aside, hoping that my touching her would give me strength to play out hell's game

of teasing our souls to the blissful heights of heaven.

Pretending not to notice Nonna Susina's protective devotion to the house her daughter had built,

I walked from room to room, and Nonna followed.

On the second floor I barged in on a family sitting around the dining table.

I frowned with true repugnance at finding strange tenants in the privacy of a home I had kept intact for years in my vivid imagination.

I was glad to see the man pale as I walked past him to check other rooms.

Nonna followed me to the top floor and down again.

She had lost a son in the First World War and had no love or trust for the likes of what she thought I was.

In the main dining room, I found the framed scenes of the Traviata still hanging in place.

Below, my own drawings were well preserved.

My two aunts, Mamma's sisters, joined Nonna, supportively scared while I set the stage for the unmasking of the intruder.

Backing up against a cupboard, where old pictures of myself and family were stuck on one side, between the glass and wood frame,
I asked my disbelieving relatives if they saw a resemblance.
Nonna, thinking I was threatening her family in America, let out tears.
I hurried to explain who I was, in the unmistakable local dialect.
The three women screamed together but were still afraid to touch me, until I removed the martial helmet that hid the individual more than it protected the head.

People gathered around the jeep, but most kept a cautious distance.
Mamma's friend, who had concluded fate had thrust her in the middle of the strange developments, kept watch by the door.
Upon hearing the screams from within, she turned toward the crowd and screamed herself before she swooned.
The onlookers, accustomed to outbursts of emotions, opened their mouths and looked at each other.
When I appeared at the door with Nonna in my arms and my aunts leaning on my shoulders, they all screamed and cried with arms directed toward heaven or clutching their breast as they moved toward us.
When the word got around which son had come home, they cried again, for me and for the other sons who might not return.

An anguished voice prevailed over the clamor of the crowd.

A black-clad, stooping figure leaned forward as she moved through the people, who made way as she approached.

With arms swung back, she moved with the posture of a diving falcon.

Unable to move her legs to keep up with her spirit, she swung her arms back and forth across her breasts, as if in self-flagellation, while crying her thanks to God.

I had never seen Nonna Marianna lose her composure, in grief or joy. I had never experienced a time when grief and joy cried together more intensely than at this reunion of spirit and flesh.

The people, the mountains and the sky generated the energy
that saturated my being with the bliss of total fulfillment.
They were the power, and I the lamp that glowed within the chamber of my senses.
The burden of life's intensity, within my bundle of flesh,
found relief in the diffusion of my self
in the fusion of spirit and matter
that made of me a part of everything
and everything a part of me.

I returned as a stranger, serving a foreign army,
part of an impersonal instrument of fear and destruction.
I came alone.
And, like any other soldier viewed as an individual,
I regained my identity of brother and son,
regardless of what flag I served.
I was a local hero.
I was of Pretare and of their blood,
involved in a war no soldier had started.
I was home.

≈

I talked to the young people as a relative they had not met.
Friends my own age were conspicuously few.
They were either prisoners of war or fighting on the Russian front.
Another dear person, the postman's daughter,
my puppy love in first grade, had died of a ruptured appendix.
In sorrow, I hugged her sisters who looked at me with the familiar, brown eyes.
Not every one was comfortable in my presence.
As a child I had been an enigma to most adults, and now,
who could guess what mischief I had in mind
for those people who might have been less than kind to my family.
The few "big shots" in town, known to be Fascists,
labored to prove how their families were related to mine.
Blood ties were not uncommon in a small town,
but I was glad to accept everyone's renewed kinship.

I had last seen Uncle Nazzareno in Ascoli when he, a sergeant and career soldier, was on his way to Ethiopia.

He had fought his last battle in Russia where he was wounded,

just in time to be discharged from the Italian Army before the Germans took over Italy.

He walked toward me with a solemn expression and a heavier limp than his condition required. He was known to use his exaggerated limp as a prelude to telling his war stories, how he was left bleeding in a Russian wheat field.

There we were! Uncle and nephew—one a committed fascist, and the other a defender of democracy.

Overlooking my uniform and the ideology it represented,

Uncle Nazzareno related passionately his personal exploits,

on the wrong side of the war I was about to rejoin.

Power may transform a meek beggar into a compassionate knight, championing the cause of weaker people.

Power is also a reminder of wrongs received.

I never realized how much I resented the town of Arquata, where its people did not work the land or practice respectable trades.

Arquata was the place where peasants brought gifts: chickens, salami or eggs, for just the promise of help from municipal clerks, lawyers, and politicians.

It was the place where all the lesser towns sent their young Balilla to march to the beat of drums, usually carried by local boys.

The center of the hill-town could be reached by car or cart,

by way of a long, winding road, or straight up, on foot.

Most peasants coming to town climbed the steep, long stairs

that caused them to bow all the way to the main square.

The people of Arquata had no idea of what a four-wheel-drive jeep could do in low gear,
let alone that anyone could drive it where people on foot labored to climb.
I still think it was worth doing, just to raise the brows of the Police Chief when he heard
the sound of a motor on the steep side of town.
And there he was!—waiting with his *carabinieri*, when I and the little mechanical monster
rolled over the last step.
The *Maresciallo* looked at my helmet, then at the letters on the jeep.
He saved face the best way he could, by saluting first, as a hint that his *carabinieri*
should do the same.
I continued my drive to the highest point of the fortress,
to convey to the town's people and to convince myself,
I had really conquered Arquata in behalf of Pretare.

A soldier learns to think of his rifle or sidearms as an indispensable part of his body.
Likewise, I grew attached to my jeep, the way a cavalry man becomes attached to his horse.
I trusted my mechanical steed, crossing bridgeless streams or speeding through a line of fire.
My jeep did not buck when I entered the smoke screen that hid the Garigliano bridge, and
I steered by dragging my foot along the edge, on the left side of the road.
It was only fitting that my reliable climber and symbol of power
be part of my pilgrimage to the green pastures
facing the rocky symbol of love and security.

The people in Pretare watched a dark silhouette move between a high ridge and the sky.
I maneuvered the jeep and my thoughts to keep a proper angle and the weight on all four wheels,
so not to lose our grip on the steep ground where only bare feet and spiked boots had ever
ventured to climb.
I climbed to give the force of reality to an idea, born of dreams and recollections.
I wanted to reconstruct the pleasure of looking down at the grounds I claimed, and still have
before me the majestic Monte Vettore for my dreams to scale.

Going to Ascoli the usual way would have been exciting enough, with four other men piled on the
jeep, had not my cousin Severino commented how the back way to the city was impassable.
He might as well have dared me!
I went for the challenge, though they all shook their heads.
But when I found the bridge gone, I conceded my jeep could not fly. I headed off the road uphill,
to look for a pass where the gorge became shallower at the base of the mountain.
At a promising site, we took the short shovel from the side of our armored mule and dug just
enough of a rut for the upper wheels to grab, as the jeep crossed, leaning sideways toward a
downhill roll. Once on the other side, five men danced around an American jeep, as fellow soldiers
on a common front.

Laughter came easily on the downhill side of the gully, as we noisily sought the civilized road from an unlikely approach.

We pushed through rocks and slid over bushes all the way to the woods, where we found a mule path to follow.

Beyond the woods, we saw a lone house with mother, father and children working in the fields.

Racing toward them, we signaled our approach by waving and yelling.

They bolted toward the house as ground squirrels scampering for their hole.

I didn't realize what a shocking sight we must have been.

From where they stood, they saw demons on wheels, descending upon them from the mountain.

The sight of civilians in flight mingled with hurt and confusion.

On the American front, civilians ran toward us.

My friends kept on laughing, a laugh that went beyond humor,

and I was ashamed for having contributed to their moment of power.

The men riding with me did not see the city I saw.

With renewed kinship and reverence,

I saw the place that had given me a first view of the outer world

and a glimpse of my own potentials.

Ascoli had begun to explain what I was and how I fit in the wider community of the world.

Ascoli was the stepping stone that led me to cross the neutral waters

that still separate my two worlds.

My fondness for Ascoli had a few painful barbs

that I wanted to blunt before leaving the city again.

My companions did not understand why I insisted they wait at the entrance of a large garage

while I drove in and parked the jeep in the middle of the floor.

The place was almost idle, but they were all there:

the *Capo*, the mechanics and the same two assistants.

As if pulled by a magnetic force, each man detached from his work

and, one at a time, faced the army jeep that had barged in with deliberate arrogance.

From a prudent distance, they looked with growing alarm at the foreign soldier who looked back with selective animosity.

The obvious plight of my former tormentors had a calming effect on my long-nurtured vengeance. They were still there and still playing humble, with rags in hand, ready to wipe any car for a handout.

I stabbed one, and then the other, with my pointed stare, and nailed their gaze to the floor.

The *Capo* edged toward my companions.

I spun the jeep around and intercepted him there.

Before the *Capo* could ask, I told him who I was.

When his mouth gaped opened, I took his hand in mine,

and with the other, pulled at his shoulder in a half embrace.

Before he recovered, I drove away,

with my friends boarding the jeep on the run.

War had taught me the use of tension and partial information

to stimulate and magnify love and hate, fear and trust, already present in the mind.

On my way back to Pretare, I smiled at the clear vision of the *Capo's* growing exuberance as he would tell the others what I had revealed just to him.

He would glow and expand on my hint of love and respect for him.

The others would keep their moment of fear as an unrelievable lump crowding their pride and self-esteem, as each reaped what he had sown in his conscience.

I smiled again at the realization of how far I had strayed from the sober issues of current history.

In a few days, I had forgotten there was a war.

Neither the Army's *Stars and Stripes* nor the APO mail service reached Pretare.

My mind disengaged from the reality of time that arranges events in a linear sequence and gives people conflicting identities.

I belonged to a foreign army, arrived from a faraway land

to fight for democracy in my own country.

I belonged with my fellow soldiers with whom I had come to know my native land as something more than a boot shape on the map.

I felt with the people who shared my thoughts, in any language.

I belonged to a world where birth and circumstances designated people as enemies or friends.

I belonged to both sides of a conflict, and only chance had determined the color of my uniform.

I belonged to Pretare, where time fused in present tense,

where its people were one with their own world.

Anthony
Caponi 29 July 1944
ITALY

Nonna Susina

Nonna Susina sat on my bed
While I painted her portrait
In watercolor.
A gray handkerchief
Hung loosely from her head,
Completing her peasant attire.
The coarse linen close to her face
Contained the loved image,
As if between my open hands.
Even as I traced her corrugated lines,
I knew I would never see her getting older.
I would never see her again,
Except in her resemblance
Looking back from my mirror.
I would never see her dead,
But always alive,
As the image I caressed with soft strokes
To record a love that would survive our flesh.

How fine is the line
between the going and coming of time!
The last glow of the setting sun
is but the first glory of morning
beyond the horizon.
So I thought, as night lowered its dark curtain over Pretare and I prepared
for the next act on a different stage, playing a different role.
So my mind drew its protective curtains around Pretare and its immense
backdrop of Monte Vettore to keep it unchanged in the backstage of my
mind where everything is of the past and the past is the substance that
flavors new experience.

Back to the war, I continued my life's journey
where the coming and going overlap
around a round timeless space
where the going is a continuous arrival
and the past an endless rediscovery.

EPILOGUE

The war lasted another long year, during which time my brother Damiano also joined
the war and chased Germans across France with Patton's Third Army.
Italian partisans killed Mussolini near the end of the war.
Mamma in applying for her American citizenship was asked what she thought of Mussolini.
Knowing better than to tell the truth and not wanting to lie she answered, "Mister Judge, I have two
sons in the war!" Without further questions, the judge signed the document and Mamma became an
American citizen.
My younger brother Claudio kept the war souvenirs I sent home and was proud to tell
stories about them.
Yolanda contributed to the war effort by working at the Goodyear factory,
riveting parts for warplanes.
She and Mamma cried together as they shared with each other the few letters I sent them.
Shortly after the war Yolanda and I married and wasted no time in blessing our family
with four children—two girls and two boys.

The story of my youth ends at twenty three years of age.
The making of the family man, the artist and the professsor is another story.

LIST OF PHOTOGRAPHS

All photographs owned or taken by the author, unless otherwise noted.
Photographs of Pretare were taken between 1944 and 1960 when the town was still unchanged.
Fascist propaganda leaflets and newspaper clippings from the author's war collection.

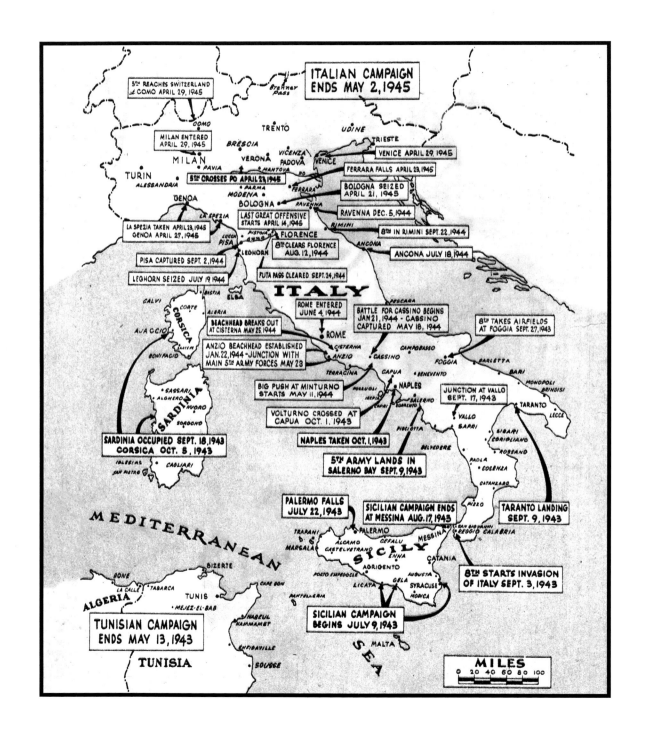